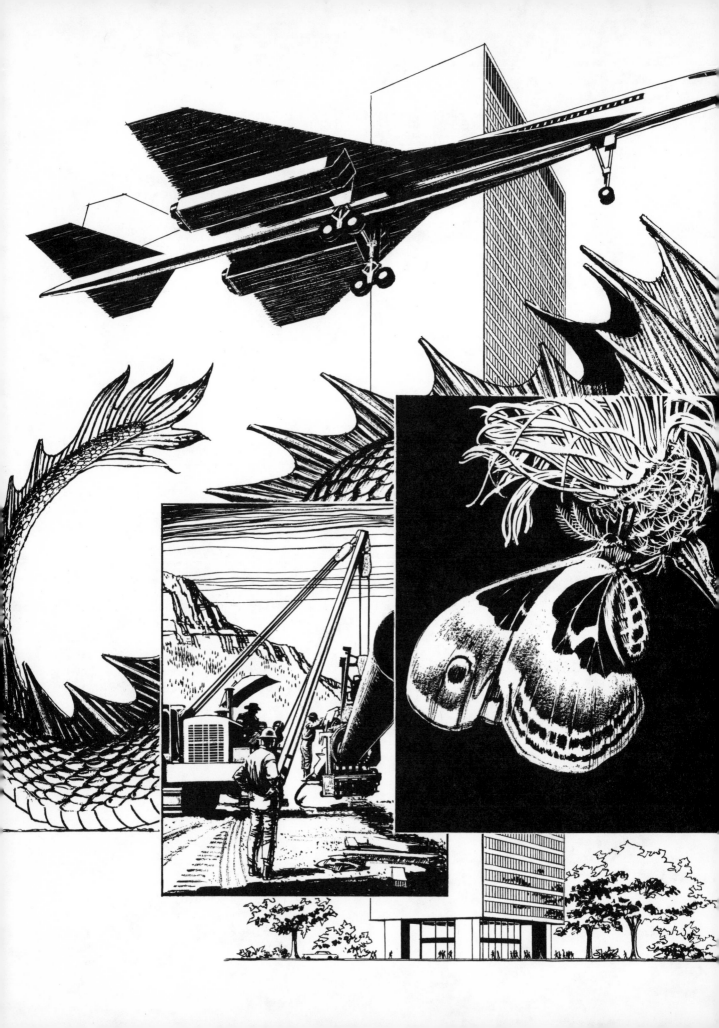

STILL MORE
Answers

By Mary Elting

Illustrated by Glen Fleischmann

GROSSET & DUNLAP   •   Publishers   •   NEW YORK

1977 PRINTING
ISBN: 0-448-02812-3 (Trade Edition)
ISBN: 0-448-03737-8 (Library Edition)

Library of Congress Catalog Card Number: 75-122566

CONTENTS

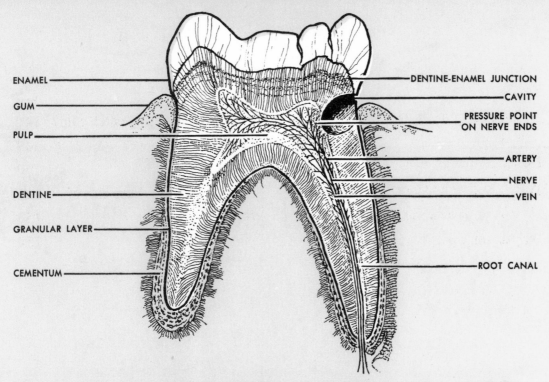

ENAMEL ——————————

GUM ——————————

PULP ——————————

DENTINE ——————————

GRANULAR LAYER ——————————

CEMENTUM ——————————

—————————— DENTINE-ENAMEL JUNCTION

—————————— CAVITY

—————————— PRESSURE POINT ON NERVE ENDS

—————————— ARTERY

—————————— NERVE

—————————— VEIN

—————————— ROOT CANAL

WHY DO HOLES IN TEETH MAKE THEM HURT?

A TOOTH is made of two substances. The outside, which you can see, is a hard, white stuff called enamel. It forms a cover for the rest of the tooth which is yellowish and something like bone.

The yellow, bony part of a tooth has a hollow space inside, and into that space run tiny living threads called nerves. The nerves connect the tooth with your brain. Now, when something irritates the tips of the threads inside a tooth, a message flashes along the nerve to the brain, and in a split second you say, "That hurts!"

The hard white outside coat — the enamel — helps to protect the nerve endings. The bony layer does, too. But if a hole forms in these coverings, trouble can start. Cold food, hot food, even cool air in your mouth may irritate the nerves. When the dentist mends the tooth, his tools may touch a nerve and cause pain.

If a hole in a tooth is not mended, germs will reach the soft inside part where the nerve is. Germs may cause the soft material to swell up and press against the nerve. It is as if you had a pimple or a boil inside the tooth, and this can be very painful indeed.

So it is not really the hole that makes the tooth hurt — it is what goes into the hole!

11

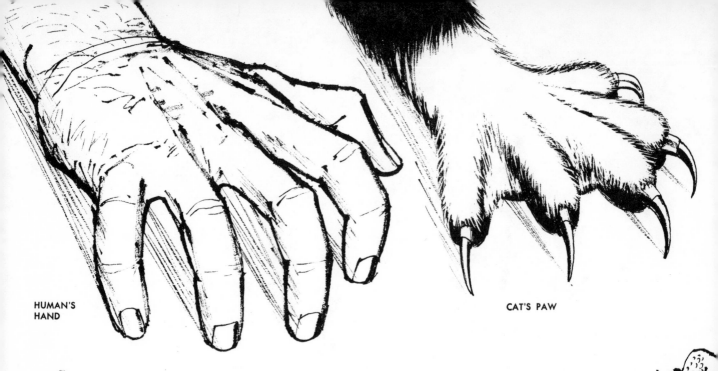

HUMAN'S HAND

CAT'S PAW

HORSE'S HOOF

COW'S HOOF

BAT'S HAND

MOUSE'S PAW

BEAR'S PAW

DUCK'S FOOT

EAGLE'S FOOT

WHY DO FINGERNAILS GROW?

EVERY DAY your fingernails get a little longer, and once in a while you have to cut them or file them down. You say that your nails have been growing, and that is true. But here is the surprising thing: the fingernails that you see and cut are *not* growing. They are not even alive. The living growing part of the nail is hidden beneath the skin of your finger.

How can the dead part of nails get longer? To answer that, we first have to find out about the living nail. If you could look at it through a microscope, you would see that it is made of tiny bits of material packed closely together. These bits are called cells. Each living cell takes in food, which is brought to it through very tiny blood vessels in the finger. Then the cell begins to split into two parts. Each part becomes a new cell which can take in food and grow. These two new cells split, and there are now four. Of course, four take up more room than one. As the growing and splitting go on and on, the many new cells press against the older ones and push them outward.

The oldest cells die after a while, and still the living cells keep forming and pushing. When nail-cells are first pushed out from under the skin, they are white. That is why you can usually see a white half-moon at the base of the nail. Farther along, the cells become transparent, so that you can see the pinkish color of the blood showing through the skin beneath.

Fingernails prove that we are related to other members of the animal kingdom. Cats and dogs and many other animals have claws instead of nails. Horses, cows and others have hoofs. But nails, claws and hoofs all are formed in much the same way.

Hoofs and claws help animals to survive in the world, and a creature gets along better when it has claws and hoofs that can grow and replace themselves if they break or wear down. Fingernails help people to pick up small objects and to do other things, but they aren't absolutely necessary.

WHY DO BABIES CRY?

A VERY young baby usually cries because he is uncomfortable. He may be hungry. Perhaps his diaper is wet. Doctors have noticed that some babies cry more just before a storm. Muggy weather makes them uncomfortable. Or they may be bothered by something that a doctor or a mother can't even figure out.

As babies grow older, they get new reasons for tears. They cry when they are angry or frightened or when they dislike something very much. Tears are signals that tell how babies feel.

As soon as children can talk, they usually cry less. They can *tell* how they feel, and so they begin to use words as signals instead of tears. Of course, talking does not always take the place of tears. Boys and girls and grownups, too, still cry at times — and there are real things to cry about in the world.

HOW CAN ICE CREAM MAKE YOUR TEETH HURT?

EVEN if you don't have any holes in your teeth, a bite of ice cream may make teeth hurt. The nerves inside teeth are sensitive to cold. When nerves are cooled by ice cream, they flash a pain message to your brain.

You will probably keep on feeling the hurt even after you have swallowed the bite of ice cream. Why? Because the whole tooth has been cooled, and it takes a while to warm up. Meantime, the nerve keeps on flashing the cold-pain message.

WHAT IS A DAYDREAM?

AN ORDINARY DREAM — the kind you have at night — is like a story. Without trying, you tell it to yourself while you are asleep, and you imagine the pictures for it, too. A picture-story that comes to you while you are awake is a daydream. You may be sitting quietly, and suddenly ideas pop into your head. They may seem so real and so interesting that you don't hear or see what is going on in the room around you. Sometimes it is fun to remember your daydream stories and write them down. Writers and painters often find they can use their daydreams when they create stories and pictures.

14

WHAT IS A NIGHTMARE?

A NIGHTMARE is an especially scary dream. Usually people have nightmares when something has been bothering them or frightening them. But they don't always dream about the exact things that trouble them. In fact, a nightmare scare is usually different from the real scare. Once a boy had a nightmare about a wicked witch. He was really afraid of an unfriendly baby sitter!

A long time ago people thought that bad dreams were caused by a kind of goblin called a *mare*. These *mares* only roamed around after dark, and so they were *nightmares*. Later, when people stopped believing in goblins, the bad dream itself was called a nightmare.

WHY DO SOME PEOPLE LIKE FOODS THAT OTHERS HATE?

ARE YOU the only one in your family who doesn't like fish? Perhaps you love orange soda and your best friend hates it. Almost everyone has strong feelings against one or two foods at least.

Many of these feelings start when something disagreeable happens at mealtime or just afterward. Take fish, for instance. Everybody else in your family may have been lucky enough to eat it when they were healthy and cheerful. But suppose you were getting measles and began to feel miserable after you had fish. Or suppose you went for a ride after dinner and got car-sick. From then on, that strong fish smell might remind you of how awful you felt. The very idea of eating fish would seem unpleasant, long after you had forgotten the original sickness. You might even begin to dislike *any* food that had a strong smell.

Or take orange soda. Perhaps you had it for the first time at a cheerful birthday party. The funny bubbles in your nose made you laugh. From then on, you liked soda. But suppose you had it first in a strange house. The bubbles in your nose surprised you, and you spilled the whole glass of it. That annoyed some adult and you were scolded. You can see why orange soda might not taste good for a long while afterward.

16

As a rule, people like best the foods that their families and friends like. If your parents belong to a religious group that does not believe in eating certain things — coffee, for example, or pork — then you may dislike even the smell of those things.

Scientists once asked the girls in a big school to make a list of the foods they would not eat. Can you guess which things were most disliked? Here are a few of them: soft-cooked eggs, oysters, olives, mushrooms, heart, tongue, turnips, parsnips, pumpkin, buttermilk.

As you grow up, you are quite likely to eat more and more foods that did not seem very attractive when you were younger. You may even find that it is exciting to taste all kinds of strange new dishes.

WHY IS SOME FOOD FROZEN?

Food for people is also food for other living things called bacteria, which are so small you must use a microscope to see them. Tiny plants called molds can also live on our food.

Millions of bacteria and molds constantly float about in the air unseen. When they land on warm, moist food, they begin to grow and multiply very quickly, and soon the food is spoiled. But they are not very active if the temperature is cold enough to make you shiver. That is why you can keep food for several days in a refrigerator.

Some bacteria and molds can continue to live on moist food that is quite cold — even as cold as ice. But at very low temperatures they are all destroyed, and so food does not spoil if it is frozen very hard. Frozen food is much colder than ice.

That is why it takes so long to thaw out when you get ready to cook it.

Bacteria and molds need moisture in order to grow and increase. They may settle out of the air onto dry food, but they do not spoil it unless it happens to get damp. That is why such things as sugar, flour, cornflakes, powdered milk do not have to be frozen.

WHAT IS KOSHER FOOD?

SOMETIMES you see on a grocery store or meat shop a sign that looks like this: כשר

The letters are written in the Hebrew alphabet, and they spell the word *kosher*. In the Hebrew language, kosher means *lawful*. The kosher sign tells you that the food sold in the store was prepared by people who follow certain religious rules or laws. The story of those rules began about three thousand years ago.

At that time the Hebrew people lived in a country called Judah. (It was later called Palestine and now, Israel.) The Hebrews and their neighbors were constantly at war. Time after time Judah was invaded. Conquerors destroyed the main city, Jerusalem, but the Hebrews rebuilt it. And no matter what happened, they stubbornly insisted on keeping their own religion and on following its many rules.

At last one of the conquerors decided to wipe out the kingdom of Judah and scatter its people, who came to be called Jews although their religious books were written in Hebrew. The temple in Jerusalem was torn down. No Jew was allowed to live in the city.

Still the Jewish people refused to give up their religion. When they had no temple for worship, they held ceremonies in their homes. Since religious feasts had always been important to them, the feasts now became family ceremonies. Like almost every other people in the world, Jews had religious customs about food. These customs governed the food people ate every day and food for ceremonies and religious feasts as well.

The rules about meat became especially strict and complicated. For example, pork was forbidden. Certain parts of other meat animals could not be eaten. Meat could not be served at the same meal with any food made from milk. If a woman followed all the rules when she cooked, then her food was called kosher — that is, lawful.

As time went on, Jewish people did less food-growing and bought more things in stores. Still, they wanted to be sure they were getting the kind of food that their religious laws called for. They could tell where to

18

buy what they wanted if they saw the word "kosher" written in Hebrew letters on store windows or on signs above doors. Today the word "kosher" may also be printed on packaged goods. These foods, too, are kosher because the manufacturer followed the religious laws in preparing them.

Many people now believe they can be Jewish without obeying all of the food rules. But many other Jews feel it is important to use only kosher food.

HOW DOES A CLAM EAT?

A CLAM is a soft little creature with a hard outside shell that grows in two parts. If you try to open the shell, you have difficulty prying the two halves apart. How can food get inside?

The answer is that the shell opens up a little when the clam is at home in the water. But a strong muscle pulls the halves together again if the clam is disturbed.

Water flows constantly in and out of a clam's body. Little waving hairs keep it moving along. Although the water may look perfectly clear, it contains the clam's food — plants so tiny that you have to use a microscope to see them. These microscopic plants get caught on special sticky waving hairs which push the food to the mouth.

Clams are sometimes called shellfish. So are oysters, scallops and mussels, and all of them get their food from the water in much the same way. Scientists have measured the amount of water that circulates through a mussel in one day — about ten gallons. There can be a great many microscopic plants in that much water.

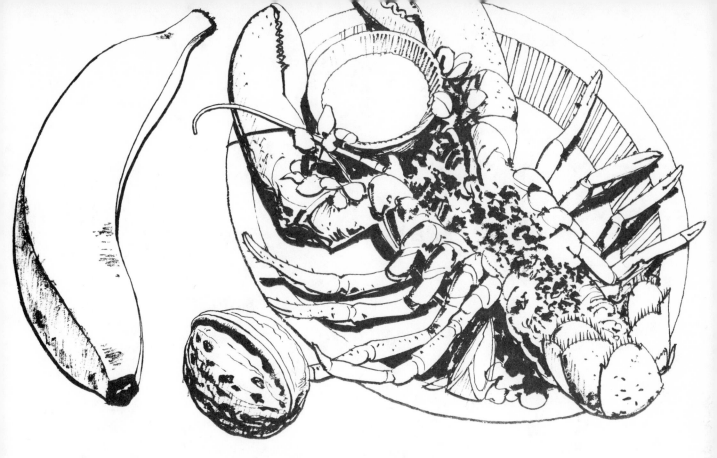

WHY DO WE COOK SOME FOODS
AND EAT OTHERS RAW?

THE FIRST men in the world ate all their food raw, because they did not know how to build fires. We could still live on raw food, but most of us prefer the taste of some things when they are cooked. Raw peanuts, for example, are bitter until they are roasted. Cooked meat has a special smell that many people like best. Sweet fruits seem to please almost everyone, whether they are cooked or not.

For a special reason fish and pork are safer to eat if they are cooked. They may be infected with worms which then grow in human beings and cause sickness.

Wheat and corn and other cereals do not give a human being much nourishment if they are eaten raw. They have to be boiled or popped or made into bread or cake. Instead of cereals, some South American Indians use another starchy food, called manioc. One kind of manioc has a bitter juice that must be squeezed out. The raw juice is poisonous, but if it is cooked, it turns into a delicious sauce!

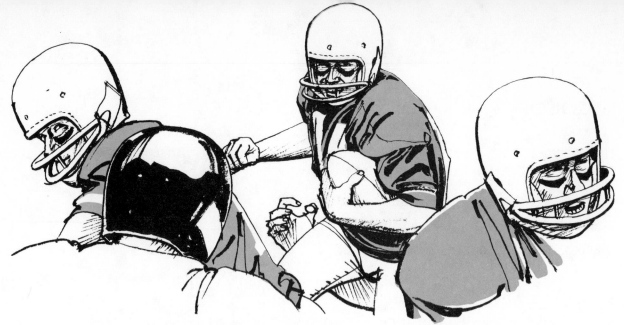

WHAT IS ENERGY FOOD?

WHEN you run or dance or play games, people say that you have a lot of energy. A scientist will tell you that energy is the ability to do work. Your body is really doing work when you play. And the energy for the work comes from the food you eat.

There are several different kinds of energy in the world. One kind is heat energy. Another is electrical. But just by looking at a bowl of cereal, would you guess that anything in it would help you to do work? Why wouldn't a bowl of sawdust do just as well?

There is energy stored up in both sawdust and cereal. It is called chemical energy. Food and wood are made of many chemicals. When you put sawdust on the fire, its chemical energy changes to heat energy. And the wonderful thing about your body is that it can use the chemicals that are in food. Inside of you, the chemical energy changes into other kinds. It becomes heat energy that makes you feel warm, and it helps your muscles to push and pull.

You need several kinds of food if you are to have a lot of energy. Meat and eggs and beans and milk, for example, help your muscles to grow. That takes time. Your body also uses some foods quickly, and these are usually called the energy foods. Sugar is one. Bread and margarine and butter are others. But here is a curious thing: if you don't eat meat once in a while — or beans or milk or egg — the energy foods may just make you fat instead of energetic!

IS COCOA THE SAME AS CHOCOLATE?

BOTH COCOA and chocolate come from the seeds of the cacao tree. These seeds, usually called beans, are dark brown and very oily. To make cocoa, men grind the beans to a powder and squeeze out most of the oil. To make chocolate, they mix some of that same oil with flavorings and other substances, and then put the powdered cocoa back into the mixture.

Plain cocoa and chocolate are bitter, but many people like the taste. Long ago a bitter chocolate drink was the favorite of Indians in Mexico and Central America. The Indians also put a flavoring made from the beans into sauces for meat. After Europeans came to the New World, they took a fancy to cocoa beans which grew on cacao trees, but they liked the taste best when the cocoa and chocolate were mixed with milk and sugar.

If you wonder why the name of the bean and the name of the tree are spelled differently, the answer is that a writer made a mistake. He was an important writer — Dr. Samuel Johnson, who published a famous English dictionary. Somehow he mixed up the words *cocoa* and *cacao* and said they meant the same thing. Actually, cocoa was the name sometimes used for coconut, which comes from a palm tree. The right name for the other tree, and for its beans, was cacao, a word based on the Indian name. But Europeans found it easier to say *co-co* than *ca-ca-o*. That is probably why they adopted Dr. Johnson's mistake. He did have the correct word for the drink that Indians made from the beans — chocolatl. That was easy to pronounce, if you left off the last letter. So we have cocoa and chocolate, both made from the bean of the cacao tree.

WHAT IS SOUL FOOD?

BEFORE the Civil War, when slaves worked on plantations, they were not given exactly the same food that white Americans ate. Suppose a hog was killed for meat. The best parts usually went to the master's kitchen. The slave cabins got the head and ears, skin, feet, insides, bones. Other foods were divided up in much the same way. Turnips went to the master, the green turnip tops were left for the slaves. Nevertheless, black women invented ways of giving a delicious taste to whatever food they had.

After slavery ended, most of the black people remained poor. Although they could often shop at grocery stores, they couldn't afford to buy all of the foods that white Americans had. So black women went on cooking the same tasty dishes, which their families liked anyway. When they could, they also cooked such things as pie and fried chicken.

Black women still make the delicious old-fashioned food, and a few years ago someone invented a new name for it: *soul food. Soul* is a word that has a special meaning for black people. It means that they have a strong feeling of brotherhood toward each other. It also means that a soul brother or soul sister is proud of being black. Soul means that black people have their own special American ways of thinking, of singing, of doing almost everything.

Soul food is food that delights black people, partly because they make it better than anyone else. These are the names of some soul food dishes: collard greens, turnip greens, hominy grits, fried chicken, corn bread with cracklings, sweet potato pie.

WHAT IS DAYLIGHT SAVING TIME?

EVERY year on the last Sunday in April, most people in the United States turn their clocks ahead one hour. The official time to make the change is 2 A.M. Suddenly it becomes 3 A.M. At this date in April, daylight normally begins between 4 and 5 A.M. But now, because the clock has been set ahead, daylight begins between 5 and 6 A.M.

During the week before this you were used to daylight ending between 7 and 8 P.M., according to real time. But tonight it does not get dark until an hour later, because the clock has been set ahead. You don't have to turn on the electric light so soon. You get more use out of the daylight. You have saved it.

In the United States, daylight saving ends on the last Sunday in October. Now you set your clock back an hour, probably before you go to bed Saturday night. Next morning, if you get up at the usual time by the clock, you will have an extra hour of sleep.

In Britain this arrangement is not called daylight saving time. People there call it summer time. In 1968 they began to use summer time all year long — even in winter.

The idea of daylight saving was adopted in Britain during the First World War. By saving daylight, people saved electricity, and this meant saving money. It also meant saving coal, which was burned in order to generate electricity. Since less coal was used, a smaller number of miners could dig what was needed. Some of the miners could become soldiers.

Daylight saving probably didn't give Britain much advantage in the war. Enemy countries adopted daylight saving at almost the same time and got the same kind of help from it. But many people found that they liked to have extra daylight in the evening after work, and so the new time has remained in use.

One argument for keeping daylight saving all year was that it would help to prevent automobile accidents. Englishmen would be safer if they could drive home before dark. True. But at the same time accidents in the dark early morning hours increased. So the total number stayed the same.

Greatly magnified cross sections of skin show the dermis, or true skin, which contains the nerves and blood vessels. Above the dermis is the epidermis, or outer skin, which has five layers. The fourth layer of the epidermis, the stratum mucosum, contains the melanin granules which color the skin.

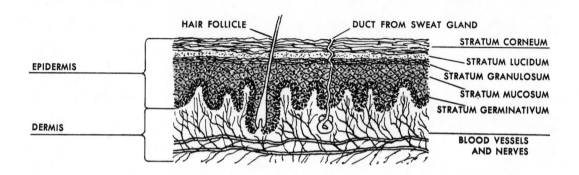

HAVE BLACK PEOPLE ALWAYS BEEN BLACK?

THE VERY first people in the world may have been dark-skinned. Nobody can be certain about this yet, because only a few bones and teeth of the earliest men have been found. These do not tell anything about the skin color of people who lived hundreds of thousands of years ago. However, we do know some facts about our own skin colors, and these facts may help scientists to figure out answers to questions about ancient man.

When you first look at skin, it seems to be all in one big piece that fits over the body. Actually, this body-covering is made up of many small parts, called cells, joined together. The cells are so tiny that you must have a microscope to tell one from another.

The microscope shows that there are several different kinds of cells in the skin. One very special kind produces tiny specks of dark-brown chemical called melanin. Now can you guess why some people have darker skin than others? Do dark people have more of these cells that produce the brown melanin? No!

Black people and brown people do *not* have any more of the special chemical-making cells than white people have! The only difference is in the amount of melanin that each cell makes. If the cells produce just a little melanin, the skin will have a very light color. If some cells produce much more than others, the skin will be freckled. If each cell produces a

26

great deal of melanin, the skin will be dark brown — so dark that it really looks black.

Scientists do not know yet why the cells behave in these different ways. Some experts think that dark skins helped ancient people to get along well in Africa where the sun is bright and clouds are few. But when men moved northward, into lands where weather is often foggy with little sunshine, those who had lighter skins got along better. Gradually the northern people in Europe became quite pale. Their skin is now almost white, but it often looks pinkish because of the red blood in the tiny, thin-walled blood vessels just below the top layers of cells.

Some northern people — those in China and Japan, for example — are neither pinkish nor dark. Their skin has a kind of golden tint. This color comes from the very thin layer of yellow fat that lies under the skin. The yellow substance in the fat is called carotene. Why do these people have more carotene than others? That, too, is a mystery that scientists are trying to solve.

IF ONE PARENT IS BLACK AND THE OTHER IS WHITE, WHAT COLOR WILL THEIR CHILDREN BE?

IF A PERSON who has only black ancestors marries a person whose ancestors are all white, their children will have a skin-color about halfway between the colors of the two parents.

If a woman who is half black and half white marries a man who is also half black and half white, each of their children will probably have a shade of color all his own. One child may be very dark. One may be very light. Others may be different shades in between. Scientists are not exactly sure why this happens. They do know that many people with white skins have some dark-skinned ancestors. Many very black people have some white ancestors. Every year more and more people of different colors marry and have children. And no matter what the color of the children's skins, they can be smart and healthy and handsome.

DID THE UNDERGROUND RAILROAD HAVE TRACKS?

BEFORE the Civil War thousands of slaves ran away from their owners. On their way to freedom they followed secret routes from one hiding place to another, and they had guides both black and white who helped them. About the year 1831 people began to call these secret routes the Underground Railroad. No one knows exactly how the name got started, but here is one explanation:

A slave named Tice Davids was running away. When he reached the Ohio River, he jumped in and swam. The slave-owner who was chasing him found a rowboat and followed. Tice Davids managed to reach the far shore — and then he disappeared. His pursuer said it was just as if the black man had found a mysterious underground road.

This idea delighted those who knew about the secret escape routes. Soon everyone was calling them the "underground road."

At this time, the first American trains began to carry passengers. The trains ran on roads made of rails, and people loved to ride on them. All over the country there was talk about the wonderful invention called the rail-roads. Slaves began to joke about riding to freedom on the secret underground *rail*road. Of course a railroad had to have *conductors* (these were the guides), who took *passengers* (the runaways) from one *station* to another. A station was a hiding place, often someone's home. The person in charge of the hiding place was the *station master*.

The imaginary underground railroad trains ran on imaginary tracks, but they carried very real passengers for more than thirty years, till the Civil War ended slavery.

HOW DO WE KNOW ABOUT TUNNEL-DIGGING IN ANCIENT TIMES?

LONG AGO, men discovered that they could dig down into rather soft earth and find the hard rock they needed for their spear points and arrowheads. Sometimes they left their digging tools in the tunnels. You can visit one such mine at a place called Grimes Graves in England.

Sometimes the top of a tunnel caved in, and an unlucky digger would get buried beneath the earth. That happened to a man hundreds and hundreds of years ago in France. His skeleton, along with his deer-antler pick, lay in the ancient collapsed tunnel until modern men, using an earth moving machine, uncovered it.

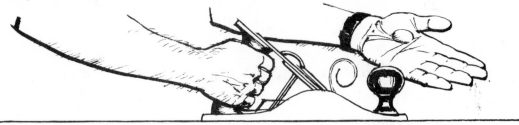

WHAT CAUSES BLISTERS?

IF YOU touch something very hot, a little bubble filled with a colorless fluid soon forms under the skin. This is a blister. Sometimes a blister forms when a tight shoe rubs against a toe or heel. And if you work hard with a tool you aren't in the habit of using, a blister may form under the spot where the tool presses against your hand.

The fluid in the blister is called lymph. (You pronounce it *lim-fff*.) The lymph moves slowly through every part of your body, in and out between the tiniest cells. Whenever any part of you is hurt or damaged, lymph comes to the rescue. It flows out and covers the burned or rubbed spot with a protecting coat that is something like gelatin when it dries. If there are germs at the injured spot, the lymph helps to destroy them.

A blister is really a kind of bandage made from the outermost layer of your skin with the healing lymph underneath it. Since it protects the hurt spot in the next layer, it is best to leave the blister unbroken.

CAN SKIN COLOR BE CHANGED?

PEOPLE who have light-colored skin sometimes make it darker by staying in the sun. They say they are getting a sun tan. Their color becomes darker because sunlight increases the amount of a substance called melanin in the skin. This substance is dark brown. As soon as a light-skinned person stays protected from the bright sunlight, the extra melanin begins to go away, and the sun tan fades.

People who are naturally brown or black already have a great deal of melanin in their skin. They can use certain chemicals to make some of the melanin disappear for a while.

So it is possible for both white people and black people to change their skin color. However, too much sun tan may cause a skin disease. Chemicals that make skin lighter can be dangerous, too.

Often black men and women have found it easier to get jobs if they had a light skin. Also, it has been fashionable for people, both black and white, to change color. Now more and more people like themselves the way they are. So they don't bother to change.

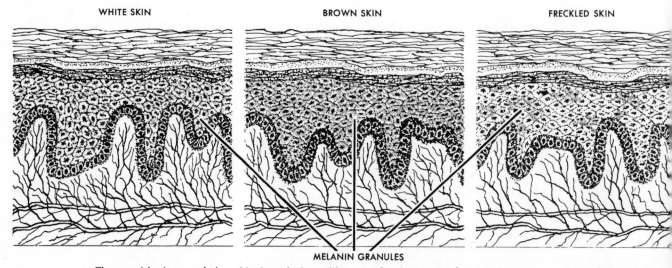

WHITE SKIN   BROWN SKIN   FRECKLED SKIN

MELANIN GRANULES

The outside layer of the skin is colorless, like a soft plastic window. It lets us see the colors underneath. In the next layer are the cells that produce the brown chemical, melanin. Just below are the tiny blood vessels with thin walls that let the red color of the blood show through. Below this are the bits of fat containing carotene. Scientists gave this yellow substance its name because they found out about it first when they were studying carrots.

30

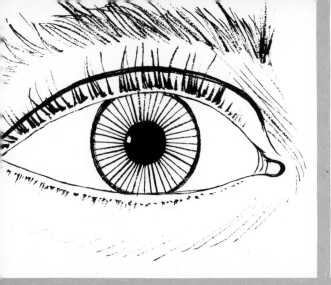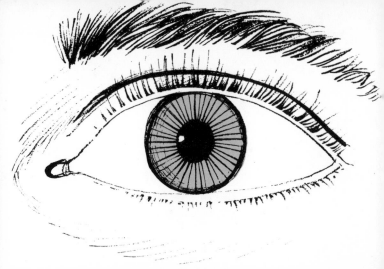

WHY DO SOME PEOPLE HAVE BROWN EYES AND SOME BLUE?

EYES get their color from a substance called melanin. This is a pigment — a kind of dye — that your body produces. The same pigment also gives your skin and hair their color. Each tiny bit of melanin is dark brown. If many bits are clustered together, your eyes will be dark brown. If there are fewer bits, the color will be light brown.

People have blue eyes for the same reason that the sky is blue! In the air overhead, tiny particles of dust and moisture are struck by sunlight, which is a combination of various colors. Most of the colors come straight through the atmosphere. But some of the blue light is scattered when it strikes the particles of dust and water in the air. The same thing happens in eyes that have only a few very tiny particles of melanin. The brown specks, too small to be seen, absorb other colors in light but scatter the blue.

WHAT MAKES HAIR TURN GRAY?

SCIENTISTS have not found the whole answer to this question. They do know that the color-making cells at the base of a hair just stop making color. As a rule this happens to old people, but not always. Some men and women have almost white hair by the time they are thirty years old. Some keep their hair color even when they are old.

WHAT IS AN EPIDEMIC?

THE ANCIENT Egyptians believed in a god they called Ptah who punished people by making large numbers of them sick all of a sudden. Nowadays we call a widespread sickness an epidemic, and doctors know that germs are to blame.

Men began to understand germs only about a hundred years ago. Before that they had many strange notions about the causes of epidemics. In the Middle Ages a terrible disease called the plague or the Black Death spread from city to city all over Europe. Almost everyone thought that it had come as a result of some kind of wickedness. Some people blamed it on the plays that were being performed at theaters. Others said it was the opera. Or perhaps it was the wild new fashion in shoes — long with very pointed toes. Or it might have been brought about by witchcraft.

In four epidemics, almost half of the people of Europe died. After that, for five hundred years, there were other smaller epidemics. At last medical men began to notice something that the Egyptians had known in ancient times: rats seemed to be connected with plague. Pictures of the god Ptah showed him with a rat in his hand.

Experiments proved that the disease does start in rats. The fleas that live on rats take plague germs into their own bodies. The fleas are not bothered by the plague, but the rats die. Then the hungry fleas move on and bite people. Through their bites the germs spread to human beings.

Nobody really knew how to cure the plague, and each doctor had his own prescription. One advised people to set dishes of fresh milk around the house to absorb the poison. Another said "Listen to beautiful songs." Another believed in keeping a billy goat in the house, so that its strong smell could drive out the disease. Still the Black Death kept spreading.

When medical men learned this, they could figure out what to do: kill as many rats as possible. Starve others by getting rid of the garbage that is their food. Keep out any rats that come in ships from countries where many people have the disease. And — most important — search for medicine that will stop plague or cure it.

All these things have been done. Now there are few plague epidemics — none at all in some countries. In many countries doctors have also ended epidemics of a disease called polio.

There are still epidemics of other diseases, such as flu, which doctors have not yet learned to stop. But at least scientists know how to go about finding the way.

WHY DO CHILDREN HAVE COLDS MORE OFTEN THAN ADULTS?

PEOPLE have been catching colds for thousands of years. But for a long time scientists couldn't capture the germ that caused a cold. They were sure it was very, very tiny — the kind of germ called a virus. If they could trap a cold virus and make it grow in a laboratory, perhaps they could find out how it worked and what to do about it. Doctors had already studied viruses that caused other diseases. Measles is a virus disease. After you have had it, you seldom get it again. Your body develops a way of fighting the germs, and the doctor says you are immune.

Then why couldn't you become immune to the cold virus? That was the mystery.

At last a scientist found out how to grow batches of cold germs in his laboratory, and before long he had some clues. There seemed to be more than one kind of virus that made people sniffle and sneeze and cough.

The fact is that any one of a hundred viruses can give you a cold. If you become immune to a few of them, plenty of others can still infect you. But the older you get the more immunities you develop. And that is why adults usually catch cold less often than children do.

LEVEL AT WHICH PRESSURE OF RISING WARM AIR EQUALS WEIGHT OF CLOUDS

WARM AIR RISING

SUN'S RAYS

HOW DO CLOUDS STAY UP IN THE AIR?

A FLUFFY white cloud floating above the earth seems very light. You can hardly believe it is made of anything so heavy as water. But of course it is. Billions of tiny water droplets drifting along together form the clouds that look like heaped-up foam in the sky.

For a long time some scientists thought that a cloud really was something like foam. That is, it was made of air bubbles surrounded by a thin film of water. Perhaps, they said, a cloud was a great collection of these little balloons, each one so small that the slight motion of wind could keep it aloft. But experiments have shown that this is not so. The droplets that make up the cloud are water all the way through. Since they are so small, warm air rising from the earth and pushing against them can keep them up.

If several droplets stick together, they form a larger, heavier drop which will start to fall toward earth. But before it falls very far, it may evaporate in the warm rising air. That is, it may separate into particles so small that they are invisible. These particles float upward with the air current until at last in higher, cooler air they draw together and form droplets again.

Clouds that stretch across the sky in very thin streaks are often different from the fluffy kind. They are made of tiny specks of ice. But both kinds are kept afloat in the same way.

WHY DOES A CLOUD'S SHAPE CHANGE?

ON A WINDY DAY the air currents may stretch a cloud out or lift parts of it higher and higher. Even if no wind seems to be blowing, warm air may be rising from earth, and it too can change a cloud. As the warm

34

air sweeps along, it makes droplets of water evaporate from the edges of the cloud. That is, the droplets fly apart in very tiny bits, and the warm air carries them away. Later, in another spot, they form new droplets big enough to be seen again. And so the cloud changes shape as it keeps losing bits of moisture in one place and regaining them in another.

WHAT IS THE VALLEY OF TEN THOUSAND SMOKES?

THERE are more active volcanoes in Alaska than in any other part of the United States, and some of them can be seen in a certain valley near a mountain called Katmai. This was a rather ordinary valley until the end of May, 1912, when the Eskimos who lived there began to hear strange rumblings in the earth. They decided to leave. A few days later Katmai cracked open, and out came great quantities of hot sand. Then the whole mountain exploded. Volcanic cinders and ash spilled into the valley. After a while cracks appeared in the valley floor, and plumes of steam and gases rose through them into the cool air. When people returned, they couldn't even begin to count the number of steaming holes. They simply called it Valley of Ten Thousand Smokes. Actually, there were many more than that — perhaps as many as a million. Most of them have now stopped steaming, but you can still see about a hundred "smokes" in the valley.

HOW DOES A BROKEN BONE GROW BACK TOGETHER?

IF YOU break a bone, the doctor is likely to say: "It will soon knit." Of course, he does not mean the same kind of knitting that people do with needles and yarn to make a sweater. The word knit also means "join together." But if you look through a microscope at a piece of bone, you will see many little loops that resemble the loops of yarn in a knitted sweater. Unlike yarn, these loops are tough and hard. They form a kind of network that gives a bone strength.

While you are growing up, the loops of bony material keep forming, making your bones larger and longer. Then, as you reach your full size, the loop-making will slow down. Your bones will not get any bigger, but they will still be able to form a new network if one is needed. Whenever a bone is broken, it needs a new network to hold the parts together. New loops soon begin to grow, criss-crossing and repairing the cracked network to make it strong again.

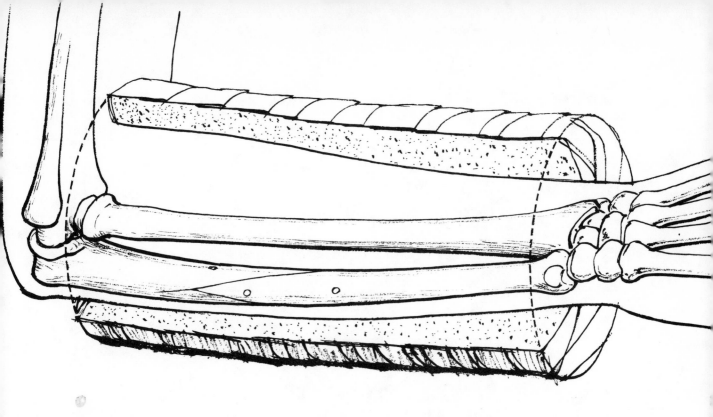

HOW DOES A CAST HELP A BROKEN ARM?

SOMETIMES, when you have an accident, a bone gets cracked, not broken all the way through. Then the doctor may just wrap the arm in a snug bandage and tell you to be careful that it doesn't get any hard jolts. In a short time the crack will be healed.

But suppose the break is complete. The broken ends are likely to wiggle around, so that new-growing bony material can't join them together. The doctor now has to make sure that the two parts stay in place. First he mixes a batch of soft, white stuff, something like modeling clay, and shapes a thick coat of it around your arm. In a few minutes the stuff hardens into a cast which holds the bone in place and protects it at the same time.

Perhaps you have heard someone say that he had to have a pin put into a broken bone, and that may sound frightening. Who wants to go around held together by a pin? You don't need to worry. First the doctor gives you a pain killer. Then he puts in a pin that is not at all like a safety pin. It is more like a small screw that holds two pieces of wood together. Usually a doctor puts in this kind of pin only when a cast cannot hold the bones in place.

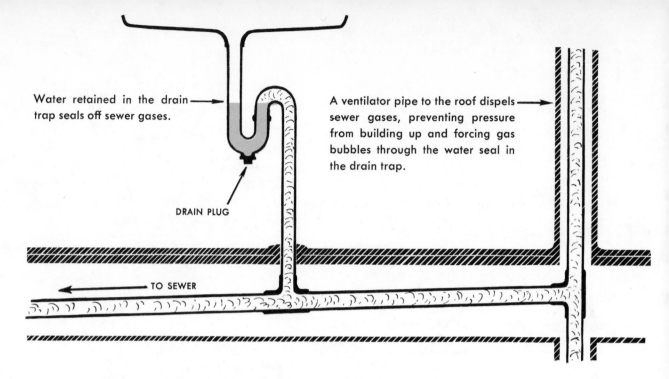

Water retained in the drain trap seals off sewer gases.

A ventilator pipe to the roof dispels sewer gases, preventing pressure from building up and forcing gas bubbles through the water seal in the drain trap.

DRAIN PLUG

TO SEWER

WHY DOES THE PIPE UNDER A SINK HAVE BENDS IN IT?

THE DRAIN PIPE under a sink looks like a letter *s* turned on its side. When you pour a lot of water into the pipe, the water travels downward, around the first bend, up over the next one, down again, and out of the house. Most of the water gets over the hump each time, but there is always a little left behind. This leftover water is very important. It forms a plug that is like a liquid door separating your house from the sewer below.

Usually the air in a sewer has a bad smell caused by decaying wastes that it carries away. There may also be a bad-smelling gas in the sewer. If very much of this gas comes into the house, it can make you sick. The plug of water in the bend under the sink keeps away the odor and protects you from sewer gas, too.

HOW DOES A TOILET FLUSH?

FLUSH TOILETS are made in two main parts. The top part is a tank that holds water. (If you can't see the tank, it is hidden in the wall.) The other part is the bowl which is connected to a drain pipe. The pipe has a hump, just like the hump in the pipe under the kitchen sink.

Now, suppose you move the handle on the tank. Water rushes down into the bowl. Then it rushes out through the drain pipe, taking with it any wastes that were in the bowl. The last quart or more of clean water that flows from the tank stays in the bowl. This remaining water is important — for the same reason that water is important in the pipe under the sink. It forms a plug which keeps out odors and sewer gases.

The toilet bowl is usually quite large. But the drain pipe that carries wastes away from it is not very big. If anything solid and large gets into the toilet, it cannot pass over the hump and down the drain. Anything as small as a bar of soap may clog the pipe and make the toilet bowl spill over into the room. That is why a toilet should not be used to get rid of anything except body wastes.

When the toilet is flushed, the water level in the tank goes down, taking the floating hollow ball with it. The descent of the ball first shuts off the flush valve and then opens the water intake valve. As water rushes in, the float rises and shuts the intake valve before the tank overflows.

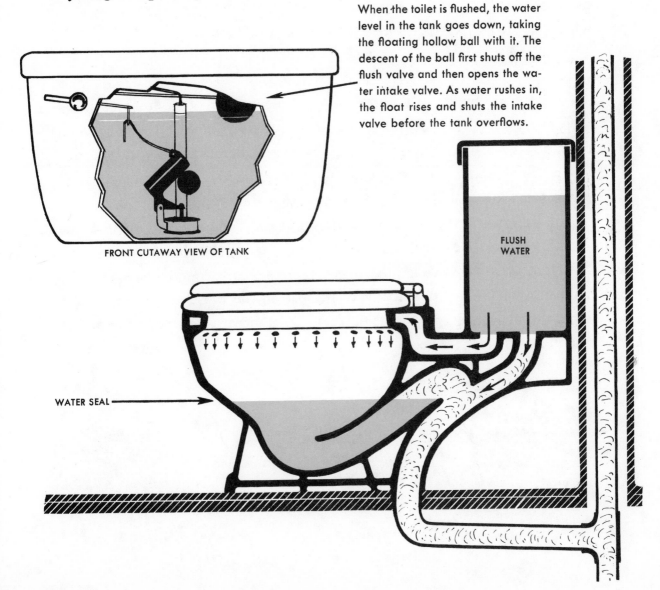

FRONT CUTAWAY VIEW OF TANK

FLUSH WATER

WATER SEAL

WHAT IS THE DIFFERENCE BETWEEN
HAIR AND FUR?

ALL OF the animals called mammals have hair. (A mammal is any animal whose babies are fed with milk from the mother's body.) When the hair is very thick and fine and silky, it is called fur. Often fur grows in a kind of double coat. The inside coat is short and curly and extra-fine. It is covered by longer, coarser hairs, called guard hairs. The underfur keeps the animal warm, and the guard hairs, which shed water easily, help to keep it dry.

The thick, very curly hair of a sheep is usually called wool.

CAN YOU TALK AFTER YOU HAVE YOUR
TONSILS TAKEN OUT?

TONSILS are small, soft lumps, one on each side of your throat, just behind your tongue. Sometimes, when you have a cold, your tonsils get red and sore. If this happens very, very often, the doctor may decide that you will be better off without tonsils. Before he takes them out, he gives you some kind of anesthetic — a medicine that keeps you from feeling pain. Afterward, the place where he snipped the tonsils away will be sore for a while. It may even hurt a little when you talk. The reason is that your voice box is close by, but lower in your throat. When you talk, there are movements in the voice box and also in the muscles of your mouth and throat. These movements don't do your sore throat any harm, and as soon as the soreness goes away, you will be talking just as usual.

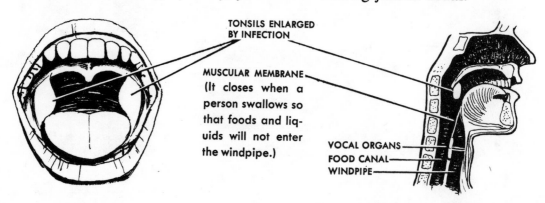

TONSILS ENLARGED
BY INFECTION

MUSCULAR MEMBRANE
(It closes when a
person swallows so
that foods and liq-
uids will not enter
the windpipe.)

VOCAL ORGANS
FOOD CANAL
WINDPIPE

WHAT IS A ROBOT?

A ROBOT is a machine that can do some of the things a man can do — and some that he can't. One kind of robot, for example, can walk; another can also pick things up with claw-like fingers. Another can work in places where there is dangerous radiation that would harm human beings. Perhaps it will some day go to explore a distant planet!

A few of these machines have been built by scientists, for fun or to use in experiments. But most of the robots exist only in science fiction stories, not in real life.

The word *robot* was invented about fifty years ago by a man who was writing a kind of science fiction play. The people in his play built mechanical men to do all their hard work. After a while these robots got tired of taking orders. So they revolted and destroyed the people who had made them.

The writer of the play lived in Czechoslovakia, and he made his word *robot* from a Czech word that means *slave*.

COLUMBUS SAILED THE *deep blue sea*
IN FOURTEEN HUNDRED *ninety-three.*

Look it up!

WHY DO WE SOMETIMES FORGET?

EVERY KIND of creature on earth can remember and forget. A worm can remember how to find its way toward food. A mathematics expert can forget his own telephone number. But even the greatest scientists don't yet know exactly *how* we recall things or forget them.

Some scientists believe that your brain is a kind of storehouse for everything you ever see, hear, feel, think or do. You don't absolutely forget anything, they say, but you can pick some memories out of the storehouse more easily than others.

How can one head possibly hold so much information? The brain is made of billions of tiny chemical parts called molecules. These molecules, in turn, make up tiny groups called cells, and the cells are arranged inside your head in an orderly way. They form whole networks, something like a living telephone system, with switches that make the connections between one set of cells and another. Special connections called nerves link your brain with your eyes, ears and other parts of your body.

Now suppose you want to remember something your eyes have read — for example, how many things make a dozen. Switches let the message travel through the network to the cells where number information is stored: a dozen is 12. Perhaps these switches are just tiny, tiny bits of a certain chemical that got jogged into place the first time you read that a dozen is 12. After that the word "dozen" jogs the chemical bits again, and they open the lines to "12."

If you forget and say "10" instead of "12," perhaps the switch or the connection isn't working properly. Not all scientists agree with this explanation, and they hope sometime to work out a better one.

42

People have done many experiments with remembering and forgetting. One experiment seems to show that if you go to sleep right after learning something you are less likely to forget it. It also seems that the pleasantest things are the ones we are least likely to forget.

Almost all scientists agree about one thing: you should not worry too much if you can't remember everything you learn each day in school. The second time you study a lesson it will be easier to remember, and you will forget less.

WHAT IS A PHOTOGRAPHIC MEMORY?

A PRESIDENT of the United States, Theodore Roosevelt, had an amazing memory. He could look at a page of a newspaper for a minute or less, then without glancing at it again he could recite exactly what was printed on the page, as if he were reading the words aloud. People often thought this was a trick with hidden mirrors or some other equipment. But it wasn't. The President had a rare ability called photographic memory.

Scientists don't understand just how people remember in this way. Somehow the memory expert's eyes and brain work together very quickly, taking in the whole picture of the newspaper page, not just individual words on it. After this "photograph" has been made, the expert can remember it so clearly that it actually seems to be held up so that he can look at it and read the words. Children are more likely than adults to have this strange ability. It usually seems to disappear as people grow up.

WHY DOES GAS IN THE KITCHEN STOVE HAVE A BAD SMELL?

ONE KIND of gas has a bad smell because there is a substance called sulphur in it. (Sulphur is what gives rotten eggs their terrible smell.) This kind of gas is manufactured from coal, and it was once the only gas that people burned in stoves.

Most of our gas today is not manufactured. It comes from wells that men drill deep into the earth. We call it "natural gas" because it was formed naturally underground. From the wells, gas travels long distances through pipes, to be stored in huge round tanks near places where people live.

Then it goes on through other pipes to homes and kitchens. If some of it happens to leak out of your stove, you say you smell gas. But you really don't. Natural gas has no odor. The odor you smell has been put into it on purpose.

There is a good reason for adding the odor. Escaping gas is dangerous. It can explode, and it can poison people who breathe it in. But because it is invisible, you will not even know it is there unless you can smell it. So the odor is added for safety. It warns you not to light a match but to open a window and get fresh air.

Gas that travels from Texas to New Jersey or to Oregon is odorless all the way, until it reaches the storage tank. There the company that sells it adds a chemical called an odorant. The odorant doesn't smell quite as bad as the sulphur in manufactured gas, but it is just as useful.

WHAT IS A MANHOLE FOR?

"MANHOLE" is a word that means just what it says. It is a hole that a man can use when he needs to fix one of the pipes or wires that run underneath the streets of towns and cities.

Manholes are covered with round iron lids so heavy that you can't get them off without a special tool. When the hole is open you can see that it is the entrance to a tunnel. The tunnels under a small town's streets may be just big enough to hold the pipe that carries sewer water away from homes. If the pipes must be inspected or repaired, the man who does the work can reach them through the tunnel.

In a big city you often see several manholes close together in every block. The reason is that many different pipes and wires run along under the streets. There are sewer pipes, and pipes for gas and water. There are cables for electric lights, and wires for telephones. The men who take care of telephones do not work on sewer pipes or water pipes, and the gas pipe men don't fix electric cables. So there must be different manholes for each kind of repairman to use.

WHAT IS FINGERPRINTING?

HOLD your hand under a bright light and you can see that the skin is covered with rows of tiny wavy lines. The lines make a kind of pattern that is very clear at the tips of your fingers. Each pattern is a little different from all the others. And nobody in the world has fingertip patterns just like yours.

These tiny lines are really very slight ridges in the skin, with valleys in between. You have skin ridges all over your body, but they show much more clearly on your fingers, heels and toes.

If you lay a finger on a piece of paper, the ridges will touch the paper, but the valleys will not. Now suppose you put a little blue ink on the finger — just enough to coat the skin without dripping. Lay the finger on the paper again. The inky ridges touch the paper and leave blue lines. In between the lines, where the valleys are, the paper remains white. Your

finger has printed its pattern on the paper, just the way the letters were printed on the pages of this book.

You can see your fingerprints when you make them with ink. But you also leave invisible prints when you touch anything with clean fingers. The invisible ink is really an oil that always covers your skin, keeping it soft. These oily prints can become visible if a special kind of powder is sprinkled on them. The powder combines with the oil and shows where the ridges touched and left their pattern.

Police make fingerprints of a person who has broken the law — robbed a house, for example. If the police find the same prints on a door or anything else in another house, they know the same burglar robbed it, too.

Some hospitals make a print with a baby's foot as soon as it is born. Since no two people have exactly the same skin patterns, a mother can check the footprint and be sure the baby she takes home is hers.

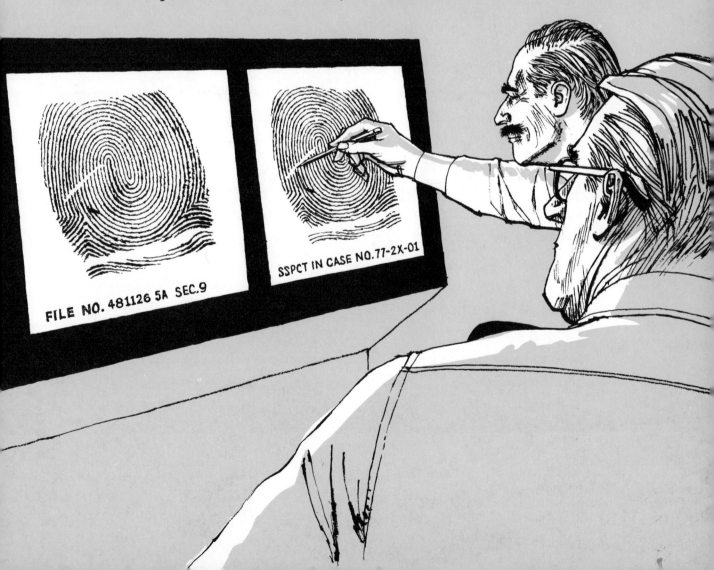

FILE NO. 481126 5A SEC.9

SSPCT IN CASE NO.77-2X-01

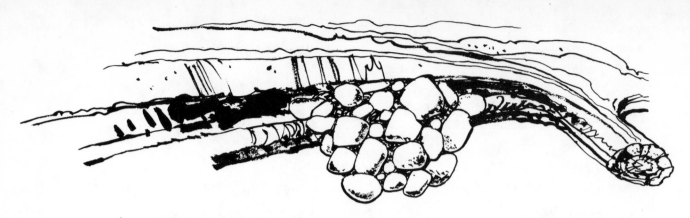

When the giant garypus (a quarter of an inch long, not counting pinchers) outgrows its shell, it spins a silken nest on the underside of a stone or a piece of driftwood and studs it with grains of sand. After the outgrown shell has cracked along the abdomen, the garypus crawls out. It lies helpless and almost transparent while its new armor forms and hardens.

DO BUGS HAVE BONES?

Bugs and other insects do not have bones. But they do have skeletons! A skeleton is a stiff framework that holds a body up. Yours is made of bone, and the rest of your body is shaped around it. An insect's skeleton is a stiff outside shell that holds the rest of its body inside.

The bones that make up your skeleton are small when you are born, and they grow until you have reached your full size. An insect is different. Its skeleton is something like a tough plastic material, and it cannot grow bigger as the insect gets older. This means that the insect has to change skeletons every once in a while.

When a young insect begins to get too large for its outside covering, a new skeleton begins to form just beneath the old one. Then the old skeleton splits apart and the insect shakes it off. At first the new skeleton is so soft that it can be stretched. Quickly, before the soft covering hardens, the insect drinks a lot of water and swells its body up with air. The new skeleton stretches, and now the insect can grow inside it. Some insects shed their skeletons several times before they are entirely grown.

HOW DOES A BALLPOINT PEN WORK?

INSIDE a ballpoint pen is a little tube-shaped tank that holds a special kind of sticky ink. When you tilt the pen to write with it, gravity pulls the ink downward to the tip. At the tip is a tiny round ball which fits snugly in a holder so that it acts like a cork to keep the ink from spilling out. But the ball can also roll around in any direction in its holder. As it rolls, the side that was inside the tank comes out, smeared with sticky ink. Now when it touches paper, some of the ink comes off onto the paper, leaving a bare spot on the ball. Around goes the ball, into the tank, and once again it gets covered with ink. This keeps on as long as there is ink in the little tank inside the pen — or as long as you don't try to write on the ceiling!

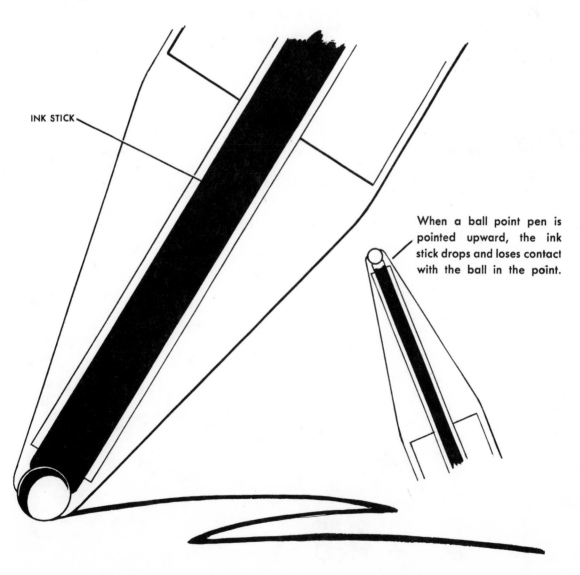

INK STICK

When a ball point pen is pointed upward, the ink stick drops and loses contact with the ball in the point.

DOES LAUGHING GAS MAKE YOU LAUGH?

THERE was once a young Englishman named Humphry Davy who liked to experiment with all kinds of chemicals. No one knew much about chemistry then — in the 1790's. So Davy was surprised one day when he sniffed a gas that he was using in an experiment. It made him very merry. Two or three whiffs, and he felt as if he were floating on a cloud. Soon after this, he had a toothache, and to cheer himself up, he sniffed some of his new gas. Again he felt carefree and jolly. And the pain went away!

Other young people heard about the experiment. For a while it was fashionable for them to have gay "laughing gas" parties. Davy went on to become a famous scientist. But doctors paid very little attention to the pain-killer he had discovered. They had always operated on patients without using anything to kill the pain, and they kept right on doing so.

Fifty years went by. Then an American dentist realized how useful the gas could be. He gave his patients whiffs of it before he pulled their teeth. From then on people suffered less when they went to dentists.

The scientific name of the gas is nitrous oxide. But "laughing gas" is much easier to say and remember. So that is what most people still call it.

WHY DOES TEAR GAS MAKE YOU CRY?

EYES are so important that the body protects them in special ways. A liquid called tears bathes them and keeps them clean. They are covered by lids that can close quickly. The lining of the lids is very sensitive, and when it is irritated by anything that might harm the eyes, extra tears begin to flow.

Tear gas is a kind of poison that makes the eyes smart. It irritates the eyelids and also keeps them from opening. Quantities of tears pour out. After a while they wash the gas away, and the lids can be made to open. Usually the gas does not do permanent harm to the eyes.

WHY DO YOUR EYES SOMETIMES STING ON SMOGGY DAYS?

A SPECIAL kind of weather brings the smog that makes your eyes sting. The air is still and damp and cool, and it stays that way for days. A blanket of motionless air hangs overhead. It gets dirtier and dirtier. There is furnace smoke trapped in it, and gases from factories, and fumes from automobiles. The car fumes contain a substance called acrolein which irritates the eyes. In ordinary weather there is usually not enough acrolein in the air to be noticed. But when the motionless air blanket traps a lot of it, sensitive eyes begin to smart.

Doctors think that acrolein and other chemicals in automobile fumes are not good for people. Fortunately there is now a law which says that new cars must be made differently from the old ones. New cars must have a special device that burns up some of the fumes instead of spilling them out into the air.

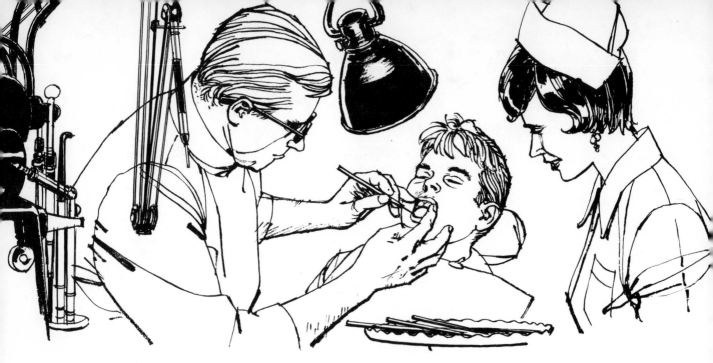

WHAT CAUSES CAVITIES IN TEETH?

IT TOOK a long time to track down the mysterious cause of cavities in teeth. Dentists followed a dozen different clues. Here are the four that finally gave them the answer:

First, germs. There are germs called bacteria which cause decay in plants and in meat. People do have bacteria in their mouths. But nobody knew of any bacteria that could eat holes in teeth!

Second, a chemical. There are chemicals called acids which can dissolve hard rocks. An acid could also dissolve the hard outside part of a tooth. But the liquid in your mouth — the saliva — isn't that particular kind of chemical.

Third, sugar. People who ate a great deal of candy often had many cavities in their teeth.

Fourth, brushing. Teeth that were brushed often seemed to have few holes.

With just those four bits of information the puzzle could be solved. This is how the facts fit together:

Saliva and bacteria in your mouth mix with food. This mixture becomes a sticky film that clings to your teeth. Now the bacteria begin to digest any sugar that happens to be mixed into the film. As they digest it, they change some of the sugar into acid. The sticky film holds the acid against your teeth, and it goes to work eating away the hard tooth material. This keeps on day after day. At last a cavity forms. If you brush the film away after eating, there is less chance that acid will be left on your teeth to make holes.

Another puzzle about teeth still has to be figured out. Why doesn't everybody get cavities? Dentists cannot say for sure. Perhaps some teeth are more easily dissolved by acid than others. Or perhaps some people have stronger resistance to the bacteria that cause the trouble.

WHAT HAPPENS WHEN YOU GET A BURN?

IF YOU hold a long-handled metal fork over a flame, first its tip will grow very hot. Then, in a little while, the end nearest your hand will feel hot, too. Heat seems to travel from the flame to the fork, and on through the metal toward your hand. How does it happen? Long, long ago this question puzzled men who thought about it, but the solution to the mystery is less than two hundred years old.

First, scientists had to discover what metal and all other substances are made of. They found that air and other gases are made of tiny flying bits of matter that they named molecules. They found that metal, too, is a collection of molecules. So are all other substances. Each molecule is very tiny. There are many billions of them in a metal fork. No matter how solid a thing is, its molecules move about. In a solid object they can't fly around as gas molecules do, but they really are in motion.

Now scientists could tell what goes on when you hold the tip of the fork over the flame. The fire gives energy to the molecules of metal, and they move around more quickly. One bumps into another and another and another. Heat energy passes from one to the next. A great deal of heat energy can jolt molecules into violent motion.

The molecules that make up the flesh of your finger will get a big, harmful jolt if you touch anything very hot. A burn is really an injury caused by millions of small, violent bumps.

WHY ARE THERE ALWAYS WARS?

THERE is almost always war going on somewhere. When warfare starts, it usually means that a leader or a group of people have decided to take something that they can't get by talking or persuading. Perhaps they want to seize good farming land or rich mining country. When this happened long ago, many groups had an excuse for taking what they wanted. Each group thought of itself as the only real people in the world. All others were unimportant, and so it was not wrong to take things from them. Today countries cannot make this same excuse.

Perhaps what people want and can't get by persuasion is freedom and equality. This kind of war is often called a revolution. Because many people in the world do not really feel free, there are often revolutionary wars.

54

The Anglo-Saxon invasion of Britain in A.D. 450.

Some people fight wars in order to make others change their beliefs. There was a time when Moslems sent out armies to kill all those who would not agree to worship their god, Allah. Then Christians went on Crusades, which were wars against the Moslems. Today men still fight wars because of religious or political beliefs.

Since the losing side in a war never likes to be defeated, there are often wars in which losers try to get back what they had to give up. In other words, wars cause wars.

The battles men fight can't decide who is right or who is wrong. They can only decide which side is stronger. And so it has sometimes happened that people avoided wars by talking and coming to agreement. The United Nations tries to stop wars in that way.

WHY ARE CLOUDS SOMETIMES WHITE, SOMETIMES DARK?

WHITE CLOUDS are fluffy. Sunshine can get through them, and the light makes them look white. But when thick, heavy clouds cover the sky, very little sunlight comes through them. And so they look dark gray. Very thick clouds may look almost black.

If you fly in an airplane *above* the rain clouds and look down on the tops of them, they are white, because the sunlight makes them bright. When you land at the airport, the undersides of those same clouds are dark.

HAS THERE ALWAYS BEEN WINTER AND SUMMER?

LONG AGO the whole earth may have been warm all year round. Certainly there was a time when the North and South Poles were not covered with ice. In those days Antarctica was a land of green forests and plants much like those which grow in the United States now. Possibly some months of each year did turn cool, but not bitterly cold and snowy.

What happened then? Why did ice begin to cover the poles? How did glaciers get started? Nobody knows. Some people think that the sun may have begun to warm the earth less than before. Or perhaps there was a change in the blanket of air which surrounds the world and helps to keep it warm. This blanket may not hold in as much heat now as it used to millions of years ago.

Some scientists believe that the ice caps will all melt thousands of years from now. Then people will wonder what winter was really like.

MASTODON MAMMOTH

WAS A MAMMOTH THE SAME AS A MASTODON?

MORE THAN 12,000 years ago the Indians in America hunted two huge animals which looked very much alike. Both kinds of animal had long trunks and great white tusks. Both went about at surprising speed on their huge legs. But it was easy to tell them apart. One kind had a sloping forehead, and it could be found in wooded country because it ate brush and tree branches. Scientists later gave it the name mastodon. The other large beast had a hump on the top of its head, and it grazed on the grassy plains. Scientists named it the mammoth.

Mammoths and mastodons were relatives — rather like distant cousins. The closest relatives of the mammoths are the elephants that still live in Africa and Asia.

All of the mammoths and mastodons that once lived in America and other parts of the world have died out. No one is sure why. The best explanation seems to be that the climate changed. The difference in weather upset their way of living. Perhaps it was too cold when their babies were born, or perhaps it was too hot and dry. Fewer and fewer of the young animals were able to grow up, and at last they all disappeared.

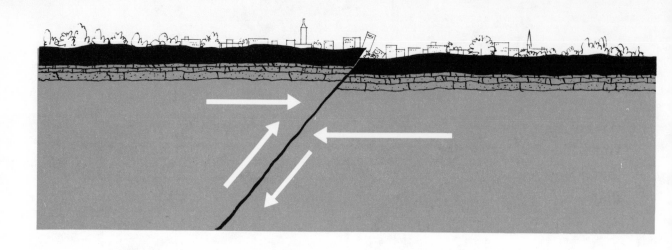

CAN YOU TELL WHEN THERE IS GOING TO BE AN EARTHQUAKE?

LONG AGO, people in Greece said that hot, damp weather — with no wind blowing — was a sign that an earthquake might be coming. Other people have said they could predict earthquakes by the position of stars in the sky or by dreams or mysterious signs. But scientists say that no one has yet worked out a true and sure way of telling when or where a quake will happen.

In California scientists have been studying one special break in the rocks which may help them to warn people that a quake is coming. This break, called the San Andreas Fault, runs north and south for about six hundred miles. The part of California on the west side of the fault has been moving northward for a very long time. Each year it shifts a few inches. This motion twists and bends the rocks under the earth. The twisting and bending go on for many years, and then suddenly the rocks split. One time when the split happened, the country west of the break jumped northward more than 20 feet! The rock on both sides of the break got a terrific jolt — an earthquake.

That quake came in 1906. Afterward scientists began to measure the yearly movement along the fault. They hoped that by keeping track of little movements they could warn people that a big one was on the way. So far, they have been able to say that small quakes might happen at certain times, but they cannot yet make accurate predictions about the exact day.

HOW DO YOU GET "SECOND WIND"?

AT FIRST, when you run fast, your breathing is the same as it is when you walk. Then you begin to gasp. But if you keep on, you lose the feeling that you must gulp in air. Soon you breathe evenly again, but more quickly than when you walk. You get your "second wind."

You don't have to think about getting second wind. A wonderful system of signals in your body takes care of your breathing speed. This is how it works:

When muscles pull your knees up and down, the muscles act something like an automobile engine. They produce wastes, just as an engine produces exhaust gases. One of these wastes from a working muscle is a gas called carbon dioxide. And this gas plays an important part in the body's signal system.

Carbon dioxide gas is swept up by blood which flows through little tubes in and around the muscles. When muscles work hard, the blood carries away more carbon dioxide than usual. In two or three seconds a special part of the brain picks up the signal: too much carbon dioxide! Immediately the brain sends out a strong signal along nerves to your chest area: breathe harder!

Now the gasping starts. With each breath, carbon dioxide leaves your body and fresh air comes in. Soon the blood is back to normal with just the right amount of the gas in it. You stop panting and take in deep, easy breaths as you run. You have your second wind.

WHY DOES A CAT FLUFF UP ITS FUR?

YOU CAN tell a cat is excited or annoyed. It flips its tail from side to side. The flipping is a sign that a special part of the cat's brain has begun to send out messages to muscles all over its body, getting it ready to pounce or scratch.

Now suppose a dog comes along and barks. Instantly that cat's tail goes up stiff and straight. Its back rises into a hump, and every hair on its body fluffs out. All of this happens because muscles suddenly tighten. The ones around its spine get shorter. They pull the backbone into an arch and hold the tail stiff. Muscles under the skin also tighten, pulling the hairs straight up.

Has the cat done all this on purpose — to frighten or warn the dog? Scientists say "No." The cat does not decide to look dangerous. Instead, that special part of its brain simply flashes an emergency message to the muscles, as soon as the cat sees and hears the dog. At the same time, other emergency signals go out to other parts of the cat's body. In seconds it is prepared for action. If it stays to fight the dog, its muscles will work well, and it can fight hard. If it runs instead, it can run very fast.

WHY DO WORMS COME OUT OF THE GROUND AFTER A RAIN?

EARTHWORMS stay underground most of the time. They live in tunnels which they make for themselves. At night they may come out to get rid of the earth they have swallowed, and they hurry back into their tunnels, if any light shines on them. But after a long, hard rainstorm, you may see hundreds of earthworms on sidewalks and streets in the daytime. They had to come out because rain seeped down into all the little chinks and spaces between particles of earth. These spaces are usually filled with air. But the rain filled them with water. Since an earthworm breathes through the surface of its whole body, it could not just poke its head out of its hole to get air.

WHY DOES A RATTLESNAKE RATTLE?

MANY ANIMALS wiggle their tails, just as a cat does, if they are disturbed or annoyed or excited. When a rattlesnake moves its tail very fast, it makes a noise like a lot of small pebbles dropping on a stone. The sound comes from the scales at the tip of its tail. Scales are made of the same kind of stuff that is in your fingernails. But these special rattling scales are attached only at one end, and so they can move. They hit against each other when they are shaken. It may seem to you that a rattler is shaking its tail to warn you. Actually, the rattling is only a sign that the snake's muscles are tightening, getting ready to strike if danger comes closer.

61

WHY DOES A WOOL SWEATER SHRINK?

THE THREAD for a wool sweater is made by twisting together the hairs of sheep. If you look at one of these hairs through a strong magnifying glass, you will see that it is not smooth. Instead, it is covered with tiny rounded scales that look something like those on a fish. You can't feel these scales when you touch the wool, because they are so small. But they are to blame if your sweater gets smaller when you wash it.

Water makes the hairs slippery. One slides over the other as you scrub the sweater. Then some of the hairs can't slide back, because the tiny scales catch onto each other. The hairs get tangled into a mass, instead of straightening out as they were to begin with. Because many of the hairs now overlap, the thread is shorter. The whole sweater shrinks a little.

Scientists have figured out a way to make wool sweaters washable. They dip the wool into a chemical which leaves a coat of soft, clear stuff on each hair. This coat is like the thinnest possible Scotch tape. It holds down the little scales and keeps them from tangling the hairs. You can scrub clothes made from this kind of wool, and they will not shrink.

Men who raise sheep have discovered still another way to smooth out the hairs. They put a certain chemical into the sheep's food. The chemical causes changes in the way in which the hairs are formed. When this wool is made into cloth, water does not make it tangle and shrink.

HOW DO MEN DIG TUNNELS?

WHEN MEN first began to dig tunnels in the earth, they had no machines to help with the work. They had only picks made of stone or deer antlers or animal bones. That was thousands of years ago. Later they discovered how to make tunneling tools of iron and steel, but the power to use the tools still came from their own muscles.

At last, a little over a hundred years ago, an inventor built a machine that helped to dig a long tunnel for railroad trains through mountains in Europe. First, the machine drilled small holes in the rock. Next, men put explosive powder into the holes, ran off to a safe distance, and waited for the explosion to break away chunks of rock. The broken rock was then loaded into little cars and hauled away.

Today men blast out some tunnels in just about that same way. The big difference is that they have better and faster drills than they had in the old days. Their explosives are more powerful, and safer. A hundred years ago the blast might go off before it was supposed to. Now it is controlled by electricity.

A new kind of tunneling machine is called a *mole*. It can cut a hole 12 feet high through solid rock — without any blasting. The cutter, which has very, very hard teeth, whirls around at high speed, chewing its way into the rock.

The "mole" (tunneling machine) shown here weighs 280 tons and is capable of boring through solid rock at a rate of 120 feet per day. The bore (diameter of the hole) is twenty feet.

HOW DID POODLES GET THEIR NAME?

MOST POODLES are simply pets. They don't work as sheep dogs do. They don't help hunters to get wild ducks. But there was a time when hunters in Germany did teach poodles to jump into the water and bring back ducks that the men had shot. Dogs that do this are often called water dogs, and the Germans gave their helpers the nickname "puddle-dogs." The word for puddle in German is pronounced *poodle,* and that is why everybody calls them poodles now.

In England hundreds of years ago, dogs helped hunters to find birds that hid in the long grass. As soon as a dog smelled or heard the birds, he stopped and crouched. Then the men sneaked up and threw a large, wide net over the grass. The birds tried to fly off, but got caught in the net. This kind of hunt was called "setting the net." And the dog that helped was called a *setter.*

WHAT IS SPRING FEVER?

SPRING DAYS bring sunshine, and the earth grows warm. Suddenly you may want to do nothing at all. In school it is hard to answer questions. "Spring fever!" says your teacher.

Spring fever isn't a disease, like scarlet fever. But it *is* a name for something real that happens to your body. You are most likely to get spring fever if you live in a place where winter is long and cold. During winter, the inside parts of your body must be kept warm, as usual. The outside parts, particularly the skin of your hands and feet, are not nearly so sensitive. Some heat can be shut off from these parts, so that the inside can have enough warmth. You probably know that heat is carried to your skin by the blood that flows through tubes called blood vessels. If the vessels become smaller, less heat is wasted through the skin. And that is just what happens during a long, cold winter. The vessels contract.

At the same time, something else happens. The blood itself changes. It now needs fewer of the tiny red cells which carry around the oxygen which the body needs for keeping warm. When spring comes, your heating system has to be adjusted. The blood vessels in your skin expand, and now the blood changes again. More red cells are needed. While they are being formed, you may feel tired and sleepy for a few days. That's spring fever.

WHAT IS AN INFECTION?

IF GERMS invade some spot in your body, and if they increase very much, you have an infection. A warm human body is a very good home for many germs. But the body also has several ways of protecting itself against infection:

The skin keeps germs out, unless it is cut or broken open.

The mouth, windpipe and lungs produce a slightly sticky substance that traps germs. If germs are swallowed, the stomach is very likely to digest them as if they were food.

Eyes have a constant bath of tears—a liquid that contains a substance that works like an antibiotic against germs.

If a germ gets through all these obstacles, it is still not safe. Very likely it will run into tiny blobs of living stuff called white blood cells. These cells never stay still. They wiggle themselves about — in the blood and in between all the muscles and among other cells of the body. When a white blood cell meets a germ, it wraps itself around the invader and digests it.

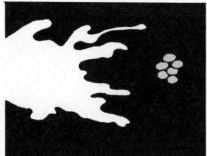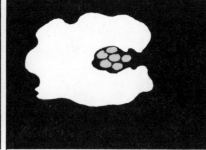

Sometimes invaders do escape all these traps. As they grow and increase in number, the infection may make you feel sick. Or it may cause a sore spot. But at the same time the white cells increase. Even without the help of germ-killing medicines, the white cells can usually bring the infection to a halt.

66

WHAT IS SUNSTROKE?

SOMETIMES, if a person works or exercises too long in the hot sun, he begins to feel dizzy. He may even faint. The doctor will probably say he has sunstroke or heatstroke. Heat from the sun, plus the work he was doing, made him sweat a great deal. At first this was good, because moisture evaporated from his body and helped to keep it cool. As he worked, the blood kept bringing water to the skin. More and more of it evaporated in sweat, and the amount of blood in his body grew smaller. Now his heart had trouble pumping enough blood to the brain. This caused dizziness and fainting. His skin felt hot and dry because the cooling sweat had stopped.

If you see anyone who has sunstroke, put him in the shade or in a cool room and call for help. Until a doctor or an ambulance comes, wrap his head in a wet towel. Get him to drink a glass of water, with a pinch of salt in it, every fifteen minutes for an hour. This will put back some of the moisture that evaporated in sweat.

67

HOW DOES A MOTHER BIRD KNOW WHICH BABY TO FEED?

WHEN BABY birds hatch from eggs they cannot fly and so they cannot go out to find food. Their parents must feed them. Suppose there are six little ones in the nest and the mother brings only enough food for three of them. Does she feed the other three the next time?

One kind of mother bird brings food to the nest and sits there until a hungry baby pecks at the tip of her bill. Then she opens her bill and drops a bit of food for the baby to pick up. Little ones that have had enough to eat don't peck at her bill, and so the food is divided pretty evenly.

Other parents behave differently. When they come to the nest with food, the hungry babies open their mouths wide and show their throats which are brightly colored. The widest patch of color gets food dropped on it first, then the next widest, and so on. A small, weak bird that has only a small color-patch may not get enough to stay alive, and it will die.

These parents are not being cruel. They simply have a feeding pattern which they are born with. The habit of giving the most food to the strongest is a pattern that has kept this group of birds from dying out. Other habit-patterns work equally well for other birds.

ARE TURTLES GOOD PETS?

TURTLES are very good pets. They are not expensive. It costs very little to feed them. And they don't make any noise that will annoy the neighbors!

A quiet turtle can't remind you that he is hungry. So you must remember to feed him. He never whines if he has a stomach ache, and you must watch him to make sure he is healthy.

You can feed your turtle a little of the same meat or fish or egg that you eat. It must be cut into very tiny pieces, because he has no teeth for chewing. If you talk to him while he is eating, he may come and take the food out of your hand, after he gets used to you.

It is not hard to keep your turtle healthy. A book about caring for pets will tell you how to do it.

HOW DO BEAVERS KNOW ABOUT DAM BUILDING?

A BEAVER doesn't really figure out how to build a dam. It doesn't plan ahead, the way an engineer does. Scientists who have studied beavers say that they just work very hard and do a lot of building. The dams that happen to be in good places will stay there, and people often see them. Nobody notices the failures.

When beavers start to build a new dam, they cut down small trees with their sharp teeth. Then they drag the wood to a stream and jam the ends of the poles into the stream-bottom. Soon they have a kind of framework from one bank to the other. Next the beavers dig up mud and plaster it against the framework of sticks. They add another layer of branches, then another layer of mud. After a while the dam is solid enough to hold water.

A pond forms behind the dam, and now the beavers can make a lodge — that is, a home of sticks and mud with an underwater entrance. The floor of the lodge is above the water level, covered with leaves and grass.

Here the parent beavers live with their babies which are called kits.

When kits are very young they need protection from cougars or other animals that might eat them. They are safest if they are protected by a lot of water. At the time when they are born, in the spring, the water in streams is usually high because of melting snow. And that is the time when grown beavers do their hardest work on their dams. A good dam makes high water even higher. So the kits are safer.

Scientists think that the coming of spring and the coming of kits have a special effect on the body of a grown beaver. Spring and new babies act like triggers which start the dam-building activities. Parents do not actually think, "Now is the time to build." They are born with the habit of acting when the trigger goes off.

Kits inherit this habit from their parents. But they also learn something by imitating their parents and other beavers. They imitate the patterns that their elders have worked out for dam building. They also learn to cooperate with others in making dams and lodges. Beaver families often stay together until the kits are several years old. Then the parents shoo the oldest kits out to make dams and lodges of their own.

WHY DO WE NEED GOVERNMENT?

SUPPOSE some people drove their automobiles on the left side of the street and others drove on the right. There would soon be a terrible traffic snarl. Nobody could get anywhere. There has to be some way of deciding which side of the street cars must use. The government decides. That's one reason why people need government.

Suppose every person who owned a piece of land could keep everyone else from crossing his property. There would be very few roads to drive on. But people need roads. This means they need a government that can make property-owners sell part of their land so that roads can be built.

Road-building costs money. Where does the money come from? It usually comes from the government, and the government gets it by collecting taxes from people. Taxes pay for roads and schools and hospitals. They also provide things like food and homes for people who can't find work. If we didn't have government, we would not have a great many things that people need.

All people need government to help them settle arguments and get along with each other. Of course we want our government to be fair to everybody. If it helps one group and hurts others, some may get angry and want a change. But they can't do away with government altogether. No people in the modern world have found any way to get along without government of some kind.

WHAT IS A GHETTO?

VERY OFTEN in the history of the world, one group of people has bullied another group who were different in some way. That happened in Europe during the Middle Ages, hundreds of years ago. In places where Catholics were the majority, they made life difficult for Jews who were a minority. Jews were not allowed to live where they wanted to live. Instead they had to stay together in certain special places.

In the year 1516, Catholics drove all the Jews out of the Italian city called Venice, onto a nearby island where there was a factory that made things from metal. The Italian word for this kind of factory was *gheto,* and the island itself came to be called the *gheto.*

Later, the spelling of the word changed, and an extra *t* was added. *Ghetto* became the name for any place where Jews were forced to live, even in countries where people did not speak Italian. Usually these places were in the most crowded and miserable parts of cities.

About eighty years ago, a great many Jews began to move from Europe to the United States. Since they were newcomers, they often wanted to live near others who had the same customs and spoke the same language. Many were very poor, especially when they first came. So they had to live in the poorest sections of cities. Soon the neighborhoods where they found homes were being called ghettos.

At first it was not easy to leave these neighborhoods, because in other parts of cities the owners of houses often refused to rent them to Jews. Later, most of the young people did move away to live in other communities. Gradually Jewish ghettos disappeared. But at the same time something else has been happening in the United States. More and more black people have moved to cities. And white people often refuse to let them rent houses or apartments except in certain areas. Blacks are kept separate, just as the Jews were on the island near Venice. And so the neighborhoods where they live are called ghettos, too.

WHY DOESN'T EVERYBODY STOP SMOKING?

SOME DOCTORS smoke cigarettes, even though they know it is a dangerous thing to do. Most of them got into the habit of smoking before they knew cigarettes were bad for their health. So did most other smokers. Now they may want to stop, but they can't break the habit.

Why is it easy for one person to give up a habit but almost impossible for another? Scientists still haven't found the whole answer. They do know that the longer anyone has smoked cigarettes, the harder it is to quit. They have also discovered ways to help people stop. One good way is to remind everybody, over and over, how unhealthy cigarettes are. Many people gave up smoking when they heard frightening TV announcements about the real danger of cancer.

WHAT CAUSES SURF?

FAR OUT from shore, ocean waves may be rounded and smooth. But closer to land they become taller and more pointed. This change is caused by a sloping beach. As a wave approaches the beach, the lower part of it begins to drag on the sloping sand underwater. Friction slows the wave down, and so water begins to pile up, taller and taller. Finally the wave tips forward. Its whole top breaks up and falls in a mass of bubbling white foam. This is surf. Of course people who ride surfboards try to keep out from under the tumbling wave-tops.

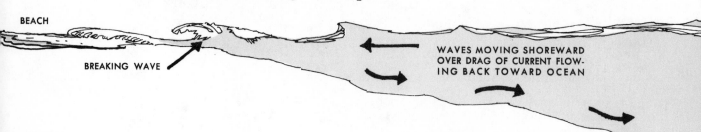

BEACH

BREAKING WAVE

WAVES MOVING SHOREWARD
OVER DRAG OF CURRENT FLOW-
ING BACK TOWARD OCEAN

The foam in surf is made up of small air bubbles. These salt water bubbles don't stick together the way fresh water bubbles do. They bounce apart and break. Each one explodes and sends water droplets flying upward. The droplets may be so small that you can't see them. But you can often taste the salt that they carry into the air.

WEIGHT PUSHING DOWN

WAVE THRUSTING UP
CAUSES FORWARD MOTION
INSTEAD OF SINKING

HOW DOES A SURFBOARD WORK?

IF YOU know how to balance on a surfboard, you can ride the ocean waves. Without paddling, you can travel at amazing speed. The board flys forward like an arrow shot from a bow.

Think about a bow and arrow, and you can see what happens when you draw the bow. The top half of a tight bowstring pulls upward. The bottom half pulls downward. When you let go of the arrow, these two pulls work against each other and give the arrow a thrust forward.

Now think of a surfboard sliding along the front slope of a wave. Gravity is pulling it downward. At the same time water is pushing upward against the board. These two forces work against each other, much like the two halves of the bowstring. And so the surfboard shoots forward, riding the wave.

Porposises often learn to ride waves just as surfers do!

WHY DO COCKROACHES USUALLY COME OUT AT NIGHT?

COCKROACHES grow best in damp, warm places where they are not disturbed. That kind of place is often dark. Sewer pipes, for example, or moist earth, or cracks near a sink in a house, are all good homes for cockroaches. Since night is the time when a house is usually dark and quiet, cockroaches are more likely to come out then, looking for food.

There are many other kinds of night insects. Some have bodies that cannot stand hot sunshine, and so they appear after dark. The bodies of others need a great deal of moisture, and the dewy nighttime is best for them. Fireflies can only find mates by looking for their flashing lights, which shine in the dark but are too dim to be seen well in daytime.

ARE RATS THE SAME AS MICE?

RATS AND MICE are close relatives. Both have sharp teeth, pointed noses, rather long tails — and very few human friends. You can tell one from the other by its size. A rat is usually much bigger than a mouse. Most of the rats that live in cities are black or brown. House mice have gray or tan fur, and they are not nearly so bold as their big cousins.

A rat is much more dangerous and destructive than a mouse. Every year rats eat or destroy millions of dollars worth of food. Because they have a tremendous appetite, they will eat almost anything. They find a good deal of food in storehouses, garbage cans, trash dumps and sewers, but they often chew their way into homes — through wood and even through cement. They will bite people if they are hungry enough. Rat bites can be dangerous. Even more harmful are the diseases that both rats and mice can spread among people.

Why don't we kill off these pests? That is easier said than done. Rats have wonderful ways of getting along in the world. They are sturdy and quick. Their families grow rapidly. One mother may raise almost a dozen batches of babies in a year. And rats are so clever that they learn to avoid many traps and poisons. Of course no rat is as clever as men, who can go to the moon and back. Probably, when men decide to have a National Anti-rat Agency, as well as a National Space Agency, city people will only find black and brown rats in the zoo.

Unlike their black and brown relatives, white rats and mice are good things to have around. They make fine pets, and scientists can use them for experiments that test certain medicines.

There are hundreds of different kinds of rats and mice. Those you see around houses in the city usually have naked tails. Others, such as the rock rat and hazelmouse, have furry tails.

WHY IS THERE CHLORINE IN SWIMMING POOL WATER?

CHLORINE is a useful chemical which kills germs. A very little of it will keep a large amount of water pure. This is important because germs in a pool could spread disease to all those who swim there. Although it destroys harmful bacteria in water, the chlorine does not hurt people.

Pure chlorine is a greenish gas. The chemist who named it was Humphry Davy, the man who discovered that "laughing gas" was a pain killer. He made the new word chlorine from the Greek word *chloros* which means *green*.

GEMS

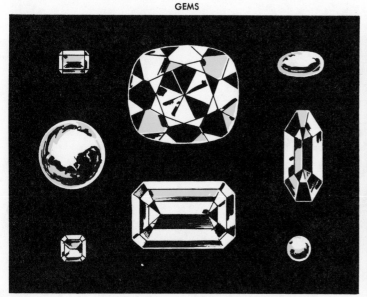

JEWELS

IS A JEWEL THE SAME AS A GEM?

USUALLY when people talk about gems they mean small pieces of colored stone that are beautiful and valuable. A jewel is an ornament or decoration which is often made of gems combined with a precious metal such as gold.

Long ago, the word jewel meant a *plaything* — a little thing to enjoy. It belongs to the same family of words as *joke,* which also means something to enjoy.

78

SCHOOL OF FISH BREAKS
LASER BEAM, REFLECTING
IT BACK TO FISHING BOAT

WHAT IS A LASER BEAM?

A LASER LAMP can send out a beam of light a thousand million times brighter than any other kind of lamp. Laser light is the strongest light men have ever made. But it travels at the same speed as ordinary light — about 186,000 miles a second.

Laser light has helped scientists to measure the distance between earth and the place where astronauts first landed on the moon. The astronauts took with them a special kind of mirror that could reflect a laser beam. They set the mirror up, and then scientists on earth flashed a beam at it. The light hit the mirror and bounced back to earth. Using very accurate instruments, the scientists figured out how many miles the light had traveled on its round trip.

A laser beam can also bounce back from things much closer than the moon. From tuna fish in the ocean, for example. Suppose that fishermen want to locate a large number of tuna swimming along together. One easy way is to hire a helicopter pilot who can fly slowly above the water with a laser lamp, flashing its beams downward. Beams of ordinary light would simply spread out in the water. But laser beams bounce back from an object beneath the surface. If they bounce from many objects moving in the same direction, the pilot can be quite sure the laser beam has located fish. He radios the fishermen, and they speed off in their boats to catch the tuna. Scientists think that fishermen should not catch too many fish with this kind of equipment. If they do, there may soon not be any tuna left.

DOES ANYONE OWN THE OCEAN FLOOR?

RECENTLY the countries of the world have begun to worry about the ocean floor. Do all countries have the right to drill oil wells in the sea-bottom? Or to mine for gold and other metals? Does any country have the right to place on the ocean floor destructive weapons that it can shoot at other countries?

Many people think that the sea-bottom is no place for weapons, but the question has not been settled. A number of countries in the United Nations *have* made an agreement saying that their borders go no farther than the line where the sea-bottom is about 600 feet below the surface. Between that line and the shore, a country can drill for oil as deeply as it chooses. It can also dig for minerals there, and it can harvest crops, such as oysters, which live on the sea floor.

The men who wrote this agreement used the word *sedentary* to describe the animal crops that could be harvested. Sedentary means "sitting." Oysters are called sedentary because the young ones attach themselves to rocks and never move away. They are in constant contact with the sea floor. That seemed clear enough. But soon two countries, Brazil and France, got into an argument about the point. Brazil said that lobsters, which lived on the bottom along its shore, were in constant contact with the sea floor. This meant they belonged to Brazil. But Frenchmen, who wanted to send fishing boats to catch lobsters, argued that lobsters did not *always* have all their feet on the bottom. Therefore they were not sedentary. The two countries continued to disagree, but they did not get into a war over a word.

WHO OWNS THE OCEANS?

No COUNTRY owns the oceans. Countries that have seacoasts do claim the right to decide what ships may sail within a certain distance of their shores. This stretch of ocean closest to shore is called the country's "territorial waters" or "offshore waters."

In the days of sailing ships, a country's territorial waters extended three miles out to sea. The reason was that a cannon on shore could shoot a cannon ball no farther than that. So there was a three-mile limit to the territorial waters that a country could defend.

Some countries still say there is a three-mile limit to their offshore waters. Others claim the right to control shipping for twelve miles out to sea. In Central America, several countries claim the right to keep other countries' fishing boats out of the seas for 200 miles from their shores.

Even in wartime, enemy countries are not supposed to harm each other's peaceful ships on the open ocean. A ship inside the enemy's territorial waters, however, is not considered peaceful.

HOW DO ANTS FIND THEIR WAY HOME?

Perhaps you have watched an ant tugging a bit of food over the ground. It goes in and out among the blades of grass. It struggles over obstacles, climbs part-way up a weed, then climbs down. The ant is on its way home. Will it get there? Or is it just wandering around lost?

Scientists have studied many different kinds of ants, and every kind has a method of finding its way home. Some ants watch for landmarks as they leave the nest. These same landmarks guide them back — just as buildings or street signs guide you home.

Some ants guide themselves by looking at the height of the sun above the horizon. People can't do this very well unless they have the help of special instruments.

Some ants can use both landmarks and the sun as guides. Scientists have proved this by experiments. First they marked an ant and followed it until it got some food. Then they picked it up and carried it around in a half-circle, so that it was on the opposite side of the nest. If the ant had been facing east before, it was now facing west. It couldn't guide itself by the sun, which seemed to be in a different place. The ant wandered this way

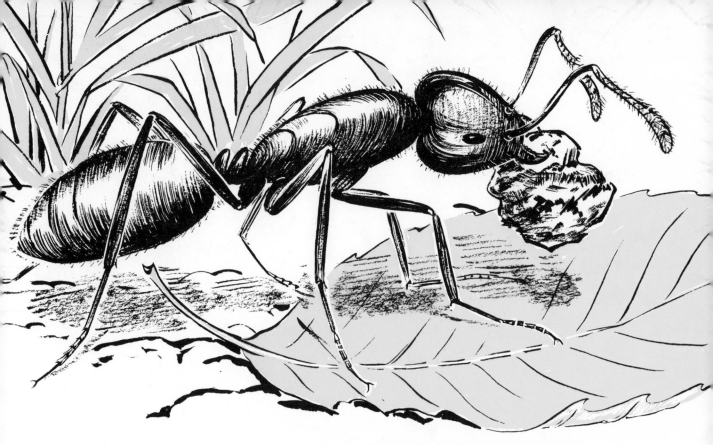

Ants have feelers called antennae on their heads. The tiny hairs are for touching and exploring. The little spots on the antennae are for smelling.

and that, but at last it found a landmark and got home safely. The scientists timed their experiments. Sometimes an ant would spend several hours looking for a landmark that guided it home.

Ants of another kind often come into houses. Perhaps you have seen them hurrying back and forth across the kitchen floor. If you look carefully, you will see that someone has dropped a bit of food and the ants have discovered it. Each one comes through a crack somewhere in the floor, takes a bite of food, then hustles away to the nest underground. There may be so many in the procession that they seem to be traveling along a highway to and from the supermarket. Yet you cannot see any special path on the floor.

These ants do not look for their path. They smell it! Watch and you will see that each one makes a stop now and then. It is pausing to drop a tiny bit of scent. Other ants can pick up the scent. And so they travel on the invisible path from their nest to the food and home again.

HOW CAN YOU BALANCE ON A BICYCLE?

WHEN YOU simply walk across the room, your body does a marvelous and complicated balancing act. Half of the time, you are standing on only one foot. You go from one position to another without even thinking about it.

This whole balancing process starts in a surprising way — with three small hollow tubes, shaped like horseshoes, inside each ear. The tubes, which contain tiny hairs, are filled with liquid. The liquid presses against the hairs, and it moves when your head moves. The slightest change in position causes a change in pressure which the hairs pick up. And they instantly send your brain a message telling about the change.

At the same time, certain nerves in all your muscles and joints are sending out messages. They notify the brain about the position of your whole body.

Now suppose that a message from the ears shows that your weight is shifting from left to right. Immediately the brain sends out messages that correct the positions of muscles and joints, so that you keep your balance perfectly. All of this happens smoothly and very fast.

When you first try to ride a bicycle, you wobble or tip over because the muscles of your body and the balance-organs in your ears have not begun to work together smoothly. But they soon begin to adjust. You find yourself making constant slight shifts of your body, so that you keep balanced on the bike.

WHY IS IT EASY TO RIDE A BICYCLE FAST BUT HARDER TO RIDE VERY SLOWLY?

WHEN YOU first learn to ride a bicycle, you may want to go very slowly. But a slow bike wobbles and tips over easily. If you lean and put a little too much pressure on one side or the other — over you go. When you ride faster, it is much easier to balance. What makes the difference? A force called momentum. Motion gives the bike momentum. The faster it goes, the more momentum it has.

A slow-moving bike has very little momentum. It does not resist when you lean to one side or steer the front wheel unevenly. But when you speed up, it takes a much stronger force to overcome momentum. Now you can steer without wobbling and lean without tipping over.

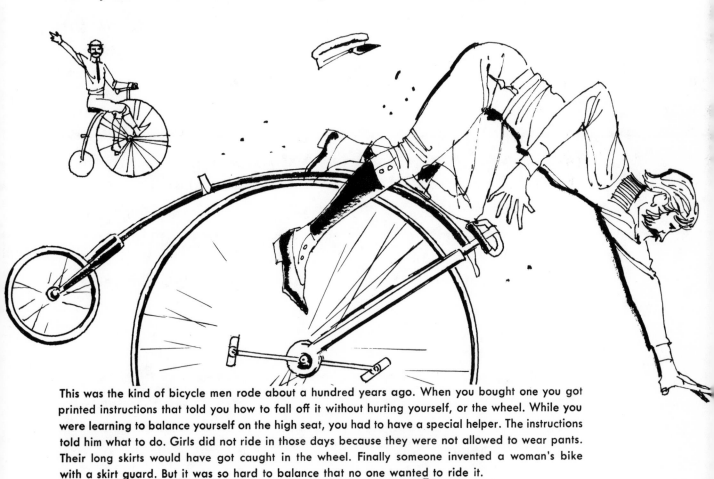

This was the kind of bicycle men rode about a hundred years ago. When you bought one you got printed instructions that told you how to fall off it without hurting yourself, or the wheel. While you were learning to balance yourself on the high seat, you had to have a special helper. The instructions told him what to do. Girls did not ride in those days because they were not allowed to wear pants. Their long skirts would have got caught in the wheel. Finally someone invented a woman's bike with a skirt guard. But it was so hard to balance that no one wanted to ride it.

WHY ARE MEN'S AND WOMEN'S VOICES DIFFERENT?

THE SOUND of your voice starts in your throat, in a special place called the voice box. This isn't really a box. It is just a wide section of your windpipe. And the windpipe is a tube that lets you breathe in and out.

At the top of the voice box are strips of tissue called the vocal cords. These cords tighten up when you want to talk or sing, and your breath makes them vibrate. The vibrations of the cords create the sound of your voice. The tighter and shorter your vocal cords are, the higher your voice sounds. Since men have bigger voice boxes than women, their vocal cords are longer, and so they talk and sing in a deeper voice.

WHY DO PEOPLE FEEL JEALOUS?

EVERYBODY feels jealous sometimes. Maybe you have an older brother who has more privileges than you have. Perhaps you are afraid your parents like him more than they like you, and that makes you angry at him. Or you may have a new baby sister who gets a great deal of attention. You feel left-out and cross. You are also scared that you will have to share with the baby some of your parents' love. Or you may have a friend who suddenly becomes somebody else's best friend. Losing a friend can make you feel angry and frightened. And that is what jealousy always is — a mixture of anger and fear.

There are many things that can make you jealous. But there are also things you can do about the problem. Sometimes it helps just to talk with another person about your feelings. You can get rid of anger by batting a ball, or by running around the block, or by cleaning up your room and tossing old junk into the garbage.

86

TOKIO
1 DAY LATER

MOSCOW
CAIRO

LONDON-PARIS
BERLIN-ROME

WHY DO SOME PEOPLE SMOKE?

WHEN EUROPEANS came to the New World, they found a strange plant called tobacco on the islands in the Caribbean Sea. There the Indians gathered the plant's leaves and rolled them into small bundles. After a bundle was dried, a man would light it and take the smoke into his mouth! In other places the Indians had pipes for smoking.

The Europeans were curious. What did the smoke taste like? They tried it, then carried tobacco home with them. Of course it amazed their friends and relatives to see them puffing at a pipe or a roll of leaves. After a while those who smoked tobacco found that they couldn't do without it. Smoking became a habit.

Today, too, some young people start to smoke cigarettes because they are curious. Others want to show off. More often, they start because their friends smoke, and they don't want to seem different. Older people almost always smoke because it has become a habit. Habits are very hard to break. But many adults *have* stopped smoking, because doctors have found that cigarettes are very dangerous. They know that certain chemicals in tobacco smoke can cause cancer and other diseases that kill a great many people every year.

Most parents do not want their children to smoke. But as young people grow up, they find that they want to be independent. They want to make their own decisions about what to do. And they sometimes can hardly resist the desire to annoy adults. Smoking annoys. So does slurping soup. But slurping is not bad for health.

87

WHAT IS ECOLOGY?

WHENEVER you see a word that ends in *ology* you can be pretty sure that it has something to do with science. Biology is a science that deals with plants and animals. Ecology does, too. But an ecologist studies something very special about living things. He wants to find out just how plants and animals get along together in the world — or why they don't get along, sometimes.

An ecologist has to be a kind of nature-detective, always looking for clues. What does an animal need to eat? What happens when its food supply disappears? How does it protect itself from enemies? Does it need a special kind of climate? Most important, what happens when the world around it changes? He asks similar questions about plants.

Fishermen used to catch millions of crayfish in the ocean near Australia. Suddenly the crayfish began to disappear. They were being eaten by hordes of hungry octopuses. Where did the octopuses come from? Some of them were gigantic, with arms nine feet long. Why had they grown so big? Ecologists solved the mystery. Fishermen, they said, had been catching too many of the sharks that live on octopuses. More and more of the octopuses escaped being eaten and grew to full size. They would keep on multiplying and gobbling crayfish until more sharks were allowed to grow and balance the food supply again in that part of the ocean.

Suppose, for instance, the fish in a pond mysteriously begin to die. Do they have a disease? The ecologist finds that the answer is "No." Are they eating some chemical that poisons them? No. Well, what about the pond itself? It gets water from a stream that flows past a brand-new town. The town has a sewage-disposal system that dumps water into the stream. That is the first clue.

Has the sewage water been purified? Yes. Still, it does have some chemicals in it. They come from detergents that are used in washing machines. What is this stuff that gets clothes clean? It belongs to a family of chemicals that makes excellent food for some kind of plants. Another clue!

Now back to the pond. People tell the scientist that the plants in it have suddenly begun to grow very fast. The chemicals from the sewage water must have been feeding them. These plants need oxygen as well as food, and the more they grow the more oxygen they take out of the pond water.

Fish, too, need oxygen. And now the mystery is solved. The plants grew so thick and fast that there was not enough oxygen left in the water for the fish to breathe. So they died.

The scientist says that the ecology of this pond was upset.

In other ponds and lakes and on land all over the world similar things are happening. What can be done? Of course people must have clean clothes, and sewage water must go somewhere. Perhaps, says the ecologist, the chemicals in detergents will have to be changed. Or perhaps better machinery for purifying water will have to be used, even though it is expensive.

Very often ecologists learn about problems only after trouble has started. But sometimes they can help to avoid trouble. Once some engineers in Siberia wanted to build a dam and make a big lake. But scientists persuaded them not to. The dam would have turned much land near the lake into a bog, and valuable trees that can't grow in a swampy place would have died. So the dam was built in a different place, and the forest was saved.

PENNSYLVANIA

MASON AND DIXON LINE, 1767

NEW JERSEY

Ohio River

EXTENSION OF
MASON AND DIXON
LINE, 1779

Potomac River

MARYLAND

VIRGINIA

DELAWARE

WHAT IS THE MASON-DIXON LINE?

OFTEN people say that the South and the North in the United States are divided by the Mason-Dixon Line. But if you look on a road map, you will not find it. The name is not printed along a line in an atlas, as the Equator and the International Date Line are. Actually, this dividing line is the border where the state of Maryland meets the state of Pennsylvania.

The name Mason-Dixon goes back to the time, before the American Revolution, when Pennsylvania and Maryland were colonies of England. For a long time the governors of the colonies had not been able to agree on the exact boundaries of the land that each of them claimed. Finally the argument was settled, and it was decided to hire experts who could measure and mark off just where the boundary line went. These experts, Charles Mason and Jeremiah Dixon, knew how to use a compass and some special instruments that helped them to figure out where a straight line would run east and west. In 1764 the men started the work, which is called surveying. They finished in 1767, after four hard years in rough wilderness country.

The line they surveyed between Pennsylvania and Maryland became known by the name of these two men — the Mason-Dixon Line. Then, almost a hundred years later, the Civil War began. Pennsylvania, which had a law against slavery, was north of the Mason-Dixon Line, and its men fought on the Northern side. Maryland did not fight on the side of the South, but people there did own slaves, and their sympathy was with the Southern side. And so Mason and Dixon's Line, which divided the two states, came to mean the division of the whole country in its feelings about slavery.

Dixie is a name often used for the South, and some people think it comes from Dixon in the Mason-Dixon Line. Others say Dixie comes from the name of a certain kind of ten-dollar bill used in the Southern city of New Orleans before the Civil War. At that time many inhabitants of New Orleans spoke French, and so the French word for *ten* was printed on the bills. This word was *dix*. People who spoke English called the bills *dixies*. When they went to New Orleans to do business and make money, they said they were going south to get *dixies*.

ANTELOPE   MOOSE   RHINOCEROS   GIRAFFE

ARE ANTLERS THE SAME AS HORNS?

THE HORNS of many animals are made of a substance called *horn*, which can develop in different and surprising ways. A turtle's shell is a horny substance. So are feathers, hoofs, fur and hair, snakes' scales, your fingernails and toenails. If you wear too-tight shoes, you may get hard little bumps called *corns* on your feet, and they are made of horn, too!

The horny growths on the head of a cow, a goat, a buffalo, a giraffe and many other creatures are hollow. If they get broken, they stay broken. New ones do not grow in their place.

The growths on the head of a deer are different. They are often called horns, but a better name for them is *antlers*. The material in antlers is bone. The bone in antlers, like all bone, is made up of a kind of network, with little open spaces. But antlers are not a hollow shell like a cow's horns. In a very special way antlers do not resemble other bones: every winter they drop off, like leaves from a tree. In early spring new antlers begin to grow.

Only the pronghorn antelope has horns of a third kind. They are hollow, but bony, and new ones grow each year. The new ones, developing inside the old, finally split the outside covering which then drops off.

The rhinoceros has a peculiar hard growth on its nose. This horn is really a tuft of hairs that develops in a stiff, upright, solid mass.

WHAT IS CONSERVATION?

THIS HAS probably happened to you: you found a nickel, then went right out and spent it for candy. Afterward you were told that you should have saved the money for something you would need or want more than candy. Maybe you agreed. Or maybe you got very annoyed at the idea of saving for the future. Either way, you had already found out about conservation.

Conservation means saving the riches of the whole world, not using them up immediately without thinking of the future. Forests, minerals, animals, water, the land itself — all these are like money in mankind's hand. They are called natural resources.

People have different feelings about natural resources. Those who own big forests often get annoyed when they are told they should not chop down all the trees to sell for lumber. Men who have ships for catching whales do not like to stop, just because there is danger that every whale in the ocean will be killed before long.

Luckily there are many people who do believe in conservation. They know that we have to use natural resources, but we must figure out *how* to use them. We must be sure there will always be something left for our children and grandchildren. For example, every time a tree is cut down, a new one should be planted. We have to limit the number of whales and seals and certain other sea animals that can be caught each year. We can't afford to let rain wash away good farming soil.

Natural resources provide things we need — things to use or eat or wear. They also provide something else that is important — peaceful spots where people can go to rest and enjoy wildlife and green growing things. Conservation means saving enough outdoor places for camping or hiking or swimming or fishing. It is also practical to save these places. Scientists need to study them. There is a great deal they want to find out about how plants and animals get along in this world. Maybe new scientific knowledge about nature will help people to get along better. And so it is sensible to keep some areas where man has not tampered with nature at all.

HOW DOES CONSERVATION WORK?

1) YOU CAN help to make conservation work. If you like a good fight, you can plan to get elected to Congress when you are older. Then you can work to pass laws that will conserve natural resources.

Fish ladder enables salmon to reach the upper level from the lower level, bypassing the dam.

2) If you like studying more than arguing, you can work in a scientific laboratory. Scientists helped to preserve salmon by studying the habits of these important fish. They found that salmon live most of their lives in the ocean. But a salmon will not lay eggs except in cool, shallow, fresh water. How could the fish reach shallow streams when dams were built across rivers? To solve the problem, scientists invented fish ladders and other devices for helping salmon to get past dams.

3) You may be able to enjoy the songs of certain birds because of a law that was passed more than a hundred and fifty years ago in Massachusetts. It protected robins and larks and other birds which hunters had almost killed off. The birds were probably saved because a writer circulated a poem he had written warning of the danger.

4) About two hundred years ago a few farmers in the United States figured out what farmers in Europe already knew: You must take care of the soil. For example, there are right and wrong ways of planting crops. If you dig the rows running straight up and down hill, rain will wash earth away into streams. (This is called erosion.) But if you plow and plant the rows around the hill — horizontally — you can stop a lot of erosion. Today many farmers know how to conserve the soil, but some still have to learn.

94

5) More than a hundred years ago some men in the United States government began trying to protect forests that belonged to the public — that is, to all of the people, not just to a person or a lumber company. But it was a long time before Congress could be persuaded to make really good laws to conserve timber on public land. On their own land, the lumber companies did as they pleased. Often they chopped down every tree. Without the shade of trees, snows melted too quickly. There were no longer any living roots to hold moisture in the soil. And so water rushed off the land and caused floods.

On public land the Forest Service now watches over tree-cutting. No one is allowed to take too much lumber from national forests. Some lumber companies also take better care of their forests than they once did. They plant new trees for the future. But some trees, such as redwoods, need hundreds or even thousands of years to grow. When lumber companies first came to California, there were millions of redwood trees. Now all but one-eighth of them have been cut and sold. Perhaps it is time to stop cutting any redwoods at all. That is what many conservationists think.

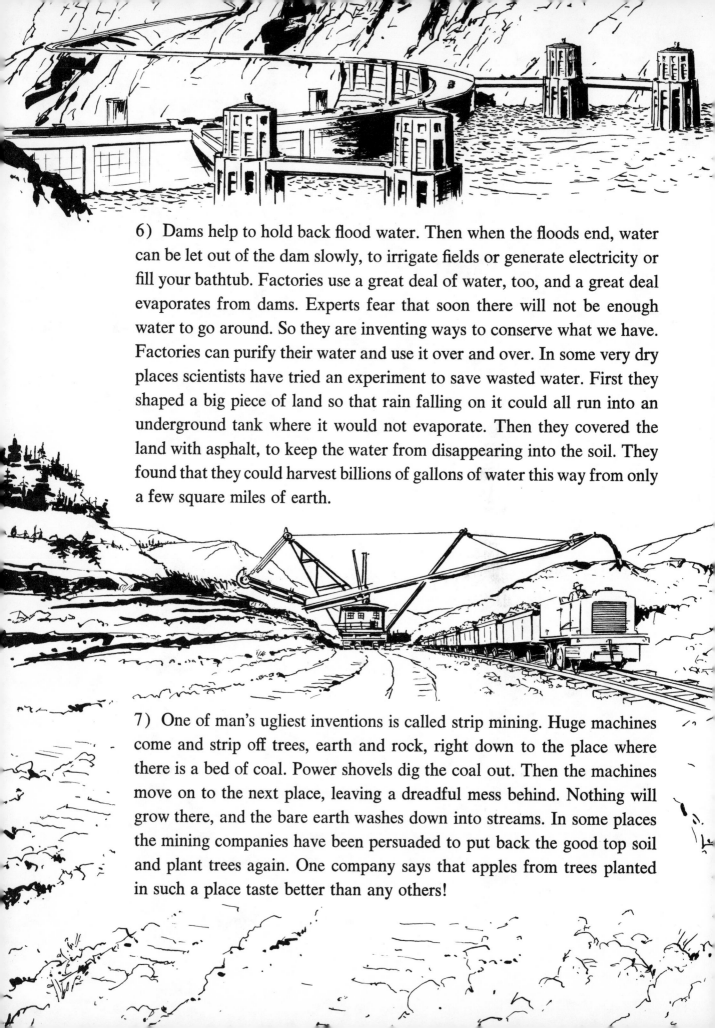

6) Dams help to hold back flood water. Then when the floods end, water can be let out of the dam slowly, to irrigate fields or generate electricity or fill your bathtub. Factories use a great deal of water, too, and a great deal evaporates from dams. Experts fear that soon there will not be enough water to go around. So they are inventing ways to conserve what we have. Factories can purify their water and use it over and over. In some very dry places scientists have tried an experiment to save wasted water. First they shaped a big piece of land so that rain falling on it could all run into an underground tank where it would not evaporate. Then they covered the land with asphalt, to keep the water from disappearing into the soil. They found that they could harvest billions of gallons of water this way from only a few square miles of earth.

7) One of man's ugliest inventions is called strip mining. Huge machines come and strip off trees, earth and rock, right down to the place where there is a bed of coal. Power shovels dig the coal out. Then the machines move on to the next place, leaving a dreadful mess behind. Nothing will grow there, and the bare earth washes down into streams. In some places the mining companies have been persuaded to put back the good top soil and plant trees again. One company says that apples from trees planted in such a place taste better than any others!

WHAT IS A SUPERSONIC PLANE?

ANYTHING *super* is bigger or higher or greater or faster.

Anything *sonic* is connected in some way with sound. So *supersonic* means faster than sound. A supersonic airplane actually travels faster than the noise it makes. To see why that kind of plane is rather special, you have to start with the sonic part — with sound.

Suppose you want to make a sound by striking a drum. The drumhead moves back and forth, and it starts a sound wave in the air around it. Particles of air close to the drum move outward, hit their neighbors and bounce back. These neighbors now hit the next neighbors and bounce back. Finally air particles close to your ear hit the eardrum, and you hear the sound. All of this happens very fast. The sound wave travels from the drumhead to your eardrum at about 760 miles an hour.

When an ordinary airplane flies overhead, a steady stream of sound waves travels outward from it in all directions. The waves reach your ear, and you hear a steady "Zoom." Since the plane travels at less than 760 miles an hour, it lags behind the sound waves that it creates.

Now suppose the plane goes faster than 760 miles an hour. Sound waves can't go out in front of it, because they have been outraced before they can form. Instead, all of the waves are concentrated into one powerful sound wave that travels behind the plane. And when that one reaches your ears, they get a tremendous jolt. This single, cracking sound is a *sonic boom*. Sonic booms can be strong enough to break windows, or make an old house collapse, and most people dislike them.

Builders know how to make supersonic planes that will travel at more than three times the speed of sound. But they don't yet know how to prevent sonic boom.

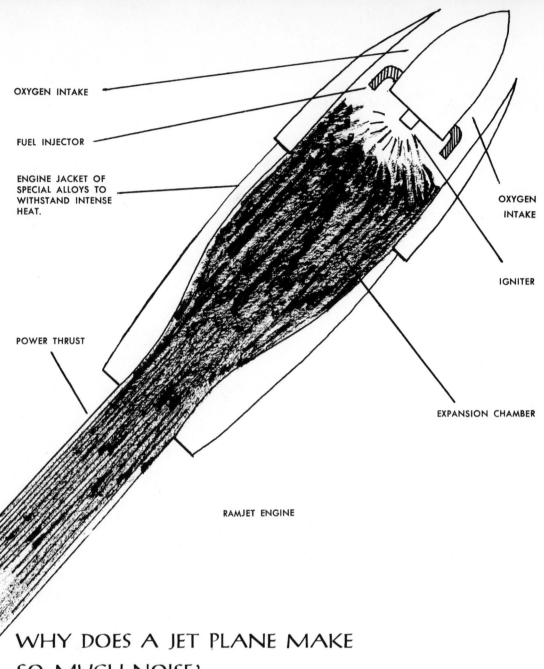

OXYGEN INTAKE

FUEL INJECTOR

ENGINE JACKET OF
SPECIAL ALLOYS TO
WITHSTAND INTENSE
HEAT.

OXYGEN
INTAKE

IGNITER

POWER THRUST

EXPANSION CHAMBER

RAMJET ENGINE

WHY DOES A JET PLANE MAKE
SO MUCH NOISE?

A JET airplane travels very fast. This means it must have powerful engines.
It may have four huge ones. Just because they are so big they make a great
deal of noise. But there is another reason for their special kind of loud
noise. First, a jet engine sucks in air through an opening at the front.
Inside the engine, the air is squeezed together — compressed. Then the air
is mixed with fuel and burned, and the hot gases burst out at the rear.
And so you hear the whine and the roar of air going in and gases rushing
out, plus the sound of the machinery which compresses the air.

98

WHAT IS POLLUTION?

IN EUROPE, more than a thousand years ago, someone invented the word pollution. It meant anything that was dirty and bad-smelling, especially the waste water from houses. In those days people dumped their slops in the streets for the rain to wash away into the nearest stream. Drinking water often came from the same stream, and it sometimes caused sickness. But nobody knew that the disease germs were spread by the slops.

Later, after Europeans crossed the Atlantic Ocean, Americans still didn't worry about getting rid of wastes. George Washington might have thought you were exaggerating if you had told him that someday pollution would spoil the beautiful Potomac River near his home. The pollution started when towns and cities grew up along the river. All of them spilled sewage into the stream. Mines and factories poured in waste chemicals.

At last a few scientists began to worry about the Potomac and other rivers. They also worried about the smoke and soot that came from factories and from furnaces in homes. What would all this dirt and evil-smelling stuff do to the world we live in? Wouldn't it spread diseases, drive away fish, poison and even kill human beings? The answer was *"Yes!"* Now the word pollution began to mean more than it had meant before. Pollution is anything that spoils the earth or the atmosphere for people and other living things.

Many modern inventions cause pollution. Some of them may surprise you. For example, loud sounds are noise pollution. Hot water poured into a river from a factory causes heat pollution. Turn the page and you will see what pollution does to the earth — and what can be done to stop it.

WHAT CAUSES POLLUTION?

1) VERY FAST airplanes can make a special kind of loud noise called a sonic boom. These booms upset people and harm buildings.

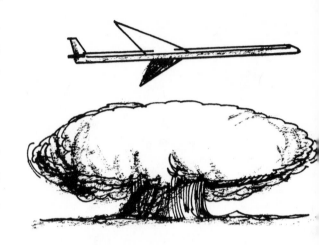

2) Atomic explosions send radioactive particles into the air. Radiation can be very harmful to living things.

3) Waste from a mine, dumped into a lake, poisons fish and may make people sick.

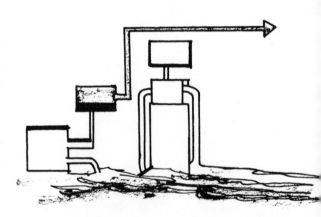

4) If farmers use too much fertilizer, rain washes some of it into streams, where it causes harm to fish.

5) Nuclear power generates electricity. It also creates great heat. The heat is carried away by water flowing into a river. Now the temperature of the river goes up, and some water-creatures die because they need cool water. At the same time water plants grow faster and clog up the stream.

6) A farmer kills Japanese beetles with a chemical poison. Much of the chemical falls on the ground, and

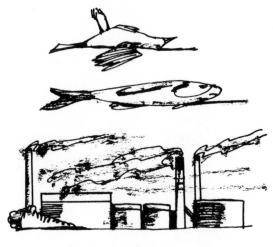

earthworms eat it. Then birds eat the worms. Although the poison scarcely harms worms, it kills birds. It kills many fish, too, when rain washes it into streams.

7) Harmful gases get into the air when waste material is burned at an oil refinery.

8) Fumes from automobiles pollute the air.

9) Factory smokestacks pour tons of dirt and harmful chemicals into the air. Smoke and automobile fumes sometimes cause smog, which is bad for health.

10) Liquid wastes from factories pollute water.

11) Sewage from the city carries germs into lakes, rivers and the ocean. The germs can spread to swimmers at polluted beaches.

12) Burning garbage pollutes the air.

13) Oil spilled from tank ships and barges kills sea life and ruins beaches.

HOW CAN WE END POLLUTION?

PEOPLE CREATE pollution, so people are the ones who must clean up our world. Scientists think that at least nine things should be done as fast as possible to stop pollution, no matter how much they cost:

1) Persuade owners of mines to dump wastes on land, not into lakes and streams.

2) Pass laws saying that all electric power plants must use a special new kind of cooling tower, instead of dumping hot water into streams.

3) Laws already say that new automobiles must have equipment for getting rid of their engine fumes. It would be even better if car manufacturers built electric cars which do not make any fumes at all. Very good electric cars have been invented.

4) Many people drive cars to work because there are not enough fast trains to carry them to and from cities. One good train will carry more people than hundreds of cars, and its locomotive will pollute the air much less.

5) Smoke and soot from factories can be trapped in giant vacuum cleaners. This will help to prevent smog. Other machinery can trap harmful

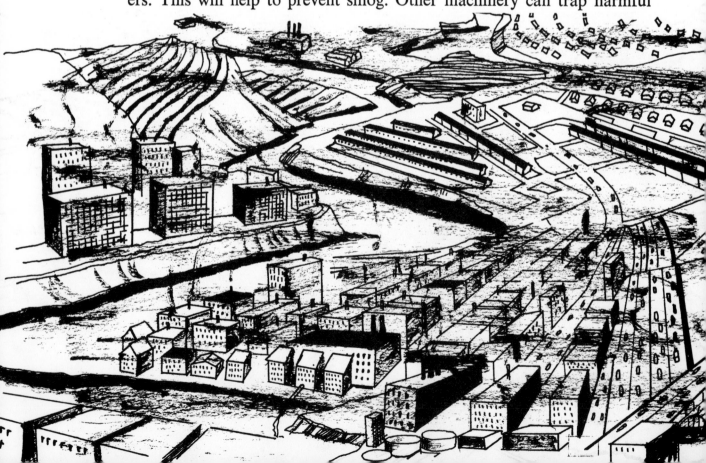

gases and make them into useful chemicals. If all this equipment is used, the factories won't need tall expensive chimneys.

6) Waste water from factories need not be poured back into streams. It can be cleaned, then used again.

7) In many places there are good systems for getting rid of sewage. These sewage disposal plants clean the water and purify it before sending it into streams or oceans. The solid material left over can be turned into fertilizer. But a great many towns and even cities do not have any disposal plants. The plants *must* be built.

8) Garbage burned in a special kind of furnace turns to cinders without polluting the air. Heat from the furnace generates electricity. Some towns have also experimented with a machine that squashes up junk, then makes it into blocks for building material. Money could pay for scientists to figure out more ways of making garbage useful.

9) Spilled oil can be sopped up in big plastic foam blankets. Then the blankets go through giant wringers which squeeze the oil out into tanks. Much oil was spilled into the ocean in one place because something went wrong in an oil well. Accidents like this can be prevented, if no one is allowed to drill a well in the ocean floor, until men have invented ways to avoid leaks.

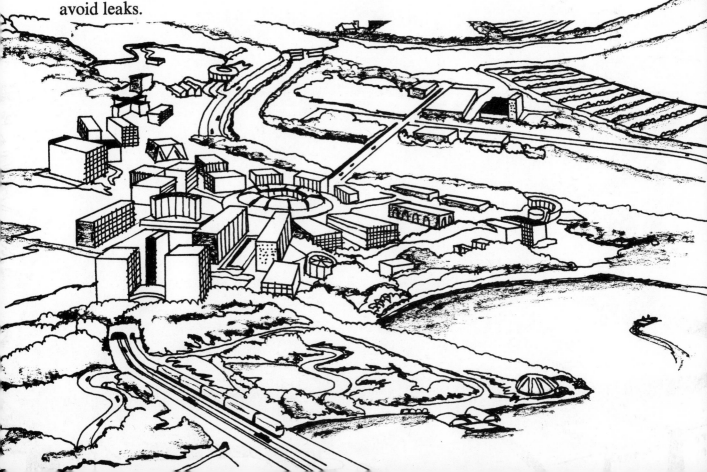

WHY DO SOME BIRDS FLY NORTH IN THE SPRING?

MANY BIRDS live in warm parts of the world all year long. In the United States these warm lands are the southern states, such as Florida and Texas. Other birds leave the southern states in springtime and fly off to spend the summer farther north. These summer visitors are usually birds that eat insects and berries, which can easily be found in warm weather. But as days get cold in the north, the insects either die or find ways of hiding and protecting themselves against bad weather. The days get shorter, too, and so a bird has fewer hours of light when it can hunt for things to eat. It would die if it did not fly away to a place where insects live the year round.

But why don't birds just give up traveling, once they have found a constant food supply in the South? Nobody knows the real answer. Some scientists believe that there wouldn't be enough food to go around if all birds stayed and raised their families in warm countries. As long as some baby birds are hatched and raised in the North, the supply of insects meets the demand.

Of course, birds didn't figure this all out. Birds cannot think and make decisions in the same way that people can. It probably took thousands of years of hit-and-miss flying before certain kinds of birds developed this regular pattern of long-distance traveling, which is called migration.

Many of the birds that live in South America migrate just as birds in North America do. But in that part of the world, the cooler land is nearer the South Pole. And so South American birds fly *south* in summer.

104

WHY DON'T ALL BIRDS FLY SOUTH IN AUTUMN?

SOME BIRDS can find enough to eat in the North, even when the weather grows cold. Several kinds eat insects in summer, but can live on seeds and the buds of trees in winter. Bluejays bury nuts in the fall and eat them when they can't find insects. Birds called nutcrackers hide pine cones, then come back to the very spot and dig them up, even when the earth is covered with snow. Owls catch mice and other small furry creatures that do not go to sleep in winter. And some birds stay near their summer homes if people put out food for them all winter.

WHY DOES YOUR HEART BEAT FAST
WHEN YOU ARE FRIGHTENED?

WHEN YOU sit still, your heart beats about 70 or 80 times a minute. That is fast enough for it to do its job. You probably know what that job is. A heart works like a pump that keeps the blood moving through tubes called blood vessels. Day in and day out, the heart sends blood to every part of the body. The blood carries nourishment, which comes from the food you eat. It also carries oxygen from the air you breathe. Most of the time you don't even notice your heart beating. It keeps on pumping because a special part of the brain sends out signals to heart-muscles even when you are asleep.

Now suppose you run down the street. Your leg muscles work hard and fast. Soon they use up much of the food that the blood has brought. They also need more oxygen. When this happens you don't have to say to yourself, "Emergency!" Instead, that special part of your brain gets a signal that food and oxygen in the blood are running low. The brain quickly sends an emergency message to the heart, which begins to pump faster. Blood flows more quickly to the hard-working muscles.

Emergency messages can also go out when you are *not* running. Suppose a truck roars around the corner and almost hits you. This happens so fast that you don't move an inch, yet your heart begins to pound, just as if you had been in a race.

Of course the truck scared you. When the danger was over, you probably thought that your heart beat faster because you were frightened. It was really something different that happened. The moment your eyes

saw danger, a signal went to some tiny parts of your body called glands. The glands instantly poured emergency chemicals into the blood. These amazing chemicals helped to prepare your body for action. They sped-up your breathing. They signaled for extra food to be poured into the blood from certain storage places in your body. They also helped to make your heart beat faster. All of this would have been a very good thing if you had really needed to jump or run.

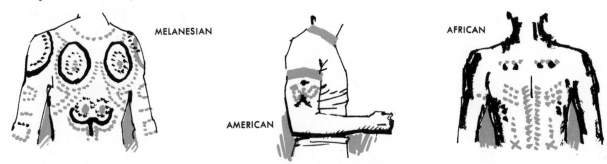

MELANESIAN

AMERICAN

AFRICAN

WHY DO SOME PEOPLE GET TATTOOED?

ALL OVER the world people love decorations. And almost everywhere there are some who like to decorate their skins. Women in America and Europe often add color to their lips or cheeks or eyelids. Many people who live in hot countries cover their whole bodies with painted designs. If they want decorations that can't be washed off, they tattoo the skin.

Our word tattoo was adopted from the language of the people on the island of Tahiti. The Tahitians made the designs on their bodies with a kind of needle that poked little bits of coloring matter under the skin.

A design may be just for decoration. Or it may show also that a person belongs to a certain group or lives in a certain part of the country. Many years ago tattoos on an Eskimo woman's chin showed that she was married. But marks on an Eskimo man's face showed how many whales he had caught!

In many countries, men and women and children all have skin decorations. In Europe and the United States, it is sailors and soldiers who especially like tattoos. Tattooing has to be done by an expert using clean needles, or sometimes the pricking can cause an infection.

Can women be elected to Congress? Yes, but more men than women are elected, and so writers almost always talk about congressmen instead of congresswomen.

WHAT DOES A CONGRESSMAN DO?

A CONGRESSMAN is supposed to help make laws that are good for the whole country. He is elected by people in his own state, but it is his job to work with congressmen from all the states. Before a new law is made, congressmen meet in committees to discuss it, and they sometimes ask experts for advice. After the committee members have discussed a proposed new law and listened to many opinions, they may decide to drop the whole idea. Or they may decide to give all the other congressmen a chance to vote for it or against it.

If people do not agree with their congressman, they often tell him so. They write letters or telephone or go to see him in his office. He is supposed to pay attention to those who elect him, even though he may not think they are right. Usually he sees that their letters or calls are answered.

A congressman often helps people by sending them information that they want. Sometimes he asks the Library of Congress to get the information. Sometimes he has it in his own office. For instance, the author of this book asked her congressman to tell her what questions young people want to have answered when they come to see him. Almost always, he said, boys and girls ask what congressmen do. One boy wanted to know this: "Can the President make children go to school on Saturdays?" You will find the answer on the next page.

CAN THE PRESIDENT MAKE CHILDREN GO TO SCHOOL ON SATURDAY?

EVERY STATE in the United States has laws that say children must go to school. In addition, every village and town and city has a committee that makes rules saying which days of the week children must go to school. These committees are called Boards of Education. There is no Board of Education that makes rules for the whole United States.

The President of the United States is supposed to work for the whole country. His job is to see that national laws are obeyed. He does not *make* those laws. However, he can make special rules if the country is in danger — if there is a national emergency. This emergency power was used years ago when many people had no jobs and the banks were running out of money. The President did make a special rule. He said that, for awhile, nobody could cash a check or take any money out of a bank.

So, unless a President decides that classes on Saturday will help out in some national emergency, the people on your own Board of Education will probably continue to make the rules.

WHY IS THE PRESIDENT'S HOME CALLED THE WHITE HOUSE?

DURING THE WAR of 1812, the inside of the President's stone house was burned when British soldiers invaded the city of Washington. At that time the United States was a very poor country. It did not have enough money in the budget to build an entirely new home for the President. So the rooms in the old house were rebuilt, and painters put a coat of white on the outside to cover up the smoke stains. People liked the way it looked and began calling it The White House. That has been its name and color ever since.

HOW DOES A FIRE EXTINGUISHER WORK?

THE FIRST fire extinguisher in the world was a rainstorm. Perhaps lightning struck a tree and made the wood so hot that it began to burn. Then came the rain. It poured on the burning tree, and two things happened: the raindrops cooled the hot wood, and they also turned into steam which spread out all around and pushed air away from the tree. Without air the wood couldn't go on burning. And so the fire was put out.

To open the nozzle of a fire hose, grasp the handle firmly and pull it back slowly. Opened suddenly, the nozzle may recoil and cause bodily injury.

Firemen still use a stream of water from a hose to extinguish some kinds of fire. (But they tell people never to put water on a burning electric wire or on burning gasoline or grease. Water on such a fire may be dangerous.) Small fires can often be put out with an extinguisher which can hang on the wall in a house or a school. You don't have to be a fireman to use it.

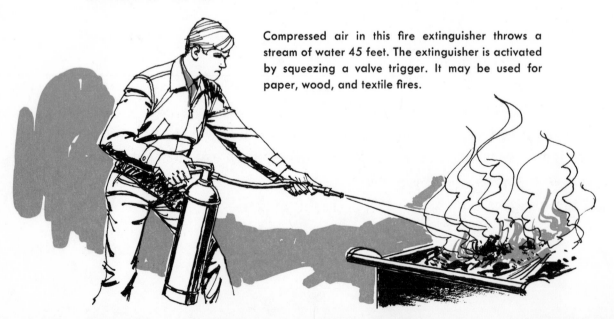

Compressed air in this fire extinguisher throws a stream of water 45 feet. The extinguisher is activated by squeezing a valve trigger. It may be used for paper, wood, and textile fires.

A soda-acid type of fire extinguisher is operated by first grasping the hose firmly and directing the nozzle toward the base of the flame, and *then* turning the canister bottom up. It is used to extinguish burning paper, wood, cloth, and organic trash.

One kind of fire extinguisher is like a big can of soda pop with a tremendous lot of fizz in it. To open the can you turn a faucet at one end, and a stream of liquid fizzes out. This liquid is a chemical that turns into a gas when it is sprayed on a blaze. But unlike the gas in the kitchen stove, it does not burn. Instead, it pushes air away from the blaze, and without air the fire dies down.

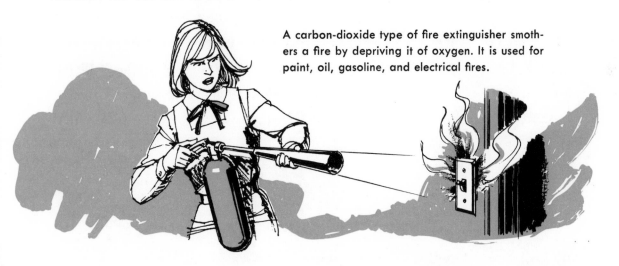

A carbon-dioxide type of fire extinguisher smothers a fire by depriving it of oxygen. It is used for paint, oil, gasoline, and electrical fires.

Another kind of extinguisher works in the same way, except that it contains a powder instead of a liquid. When the powder is squirted on a fire it produces a gas. At the same time it forms a sort of crust on whatever is burning. The gas and the crust together keep the air away, and the fire goes out.

111

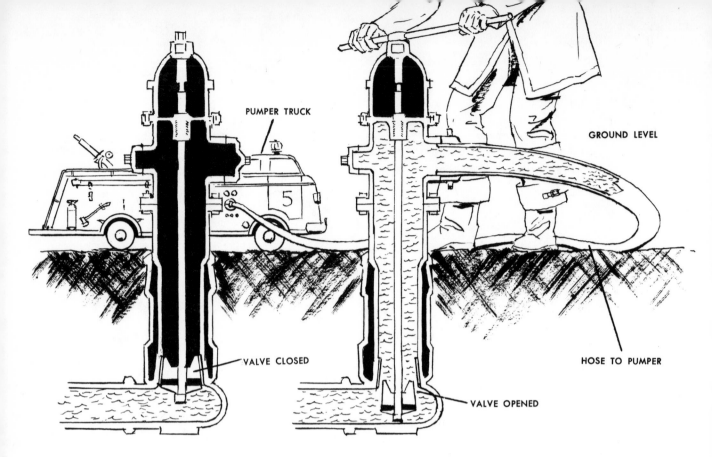

PUMPER TRUCK

GROUND LEVEL

VALVE CLOSED

HOSE TO PUMPER

VALVE OPENED

HOW DOES A FIRE HYDRANT WORK?

A FIRE HYDRANT is like a huge water faucet without a handle. When a fire-man wants to turn it on, he brings the handle with him. When he isn't using it, he keeps the handle in the firehouse so that the hydrant won't get turned on accidentally — or by someone who thinks it would be a good joke to let the water run. If the water is wasted, there might not be enough to put out a fire.

A stream of water comes out of the hydrant with great force. Still, it isn't strong enough to shoot to the top of a big building. If a tall build-ing starts to burn, firemen bring a special engine called a pumper. They attach a pipe from the pumper engine to the hydrant. Then a strong pump inside the engine forces the water out through the hose in a powerful stream that can shoot high above the street.

Before fire engines were invented, men had to do the pumping that sent water through the hose. They couldn't make it go very high. The first hoses were made from strips of leather held tightly together with metal pins.

CAN HURRICANES BE STOPPED?

WEATHERMEN would like to find a way of stopping this terrible kind of storm. But they still haven't learned enough to do so. They know that a hurricane often starts when warm moist air rises and meets air that is traveling parallel to earth. The whole mass begins to swirl around in a huge circle. But scientists aren't entirely sure why this circling air often turns into winds that can blow down trees and rip houses apart. They can't tell why a hurricane goes where it goes, or why it may suddenly change its course.

People have had many ideas about stopping hurricane winds. Why not fire guns at them and break them up? Maybe an airplane could drop a bomb into the middle of the hurricane and stop it. Could airplanes shoot chemicals into the storm and drive it away from land, out to sea where it would do less harm? So far no such plan has worked out.

Although weathermen can't stop a hurricane, they can at least see one coming. They have weather satellites to help them. These satellites are small space ships that travel in an orbit around the earth. In them are cameras, something like TV cameras, which send out pictures of clouds over land and sea. A picture of thick clouds swirling in a great circle warns the weathermen of a hurricane. If the cloud pictures show up soon enough, the weathermen can then warn people to prepare for the storm.

Someday there may be enough weather stations and satellites to give all the information that is needed to understand hurricanes. They probably can't be stopped entirely. And it might not even be a good idea to do so. Perhaps if the weather were improved in one place, it might get worse in other places. Scientists are studying that problem, too.

Meteorological satellite *Tiros III*, orbiting in space, discovered Hurricane Esther several days before the storm struck land areas.

WHY ARE SOME CLOTHES COOLER THAN OTHERS?

ON A SUNSHINY day, white clothes are cooler than dark-colored clothes. You can prove this. Get two ice cubes and cover one with white cloth, one with black cloth. The second piece of ice will melt first. That is because the sun's light and heat are absorbed by black materials. White things reflect sunshine. And so less heat reaches your body if you are wearing light-colored clothes.

Thin cloth is usually cooler than thick cloth. The spaces between the threads of thin cloth allow tiny drops of sweat to leave your body and disappear into the air. When sweat evaporates it takes heat away from your body, so you are cooler.

Crinkled cloth is especially cool. Small ridges are woven into the cloth. They touch your skin, but the cloth between them does not. This leaves a space for air to circulate, and the moving air helps to carry away sweat.

SWATCH OF SEERSUCKER CLOTH

One type of crinkled cloth was invented in India. There people called it "milk and sugar" cloth because the ridges and valleys gave it two different textures. The Indians' word for milk and sugar sounded liked "seersucker" to Englishmen, and that became the name of the cloth in England and in America, too.

Forest ranger in lookout tower spots lightning-caused fire and directs fire fighters to location.

CAN MEN PREVENT LIGHTNING?

SOME LIGHTNING jumps from clouds to earth. When it reaches earth it can start fires in huge forests far out in the wilderness. Firefighters hurry to the rescue as fast as they can. But a blaze often gets a head start before the men can put it out. Firefighting is hard and expensive work. Why not fight the lightning instead? That is just what scientists have tried to do.

First they did some experiments in a laboratory. The results seemed to show that the least dangerous storm clouds were the ones made of tiny ice crystals rather than raindrops. This gave them an idea. Maybe they could find a way to create ice particles in the clouds! So they began some experiments out of doors.

For this kind of experiment the scientists needed an airplane and a kind of blower that could send a special chemical into the rain clouds. If the clouds happened to be very cold ones, this chemical could make some of the raindrops turn into tiny particles of ice.

Again and again pilots carried up loads of the ice-making stuff. (They said they were "seeding the clouds.") And when the experiment was over, the scientists found an exciting result: much less lightning jumped from the seeded clouds than from the unseeded ones.

Some lightning can be prevented. Perhaps the time will come when cloud-seekers will keep many forest fires from starting. Of course, the experts don't all agree about stopping fires. Some of them believe that there are times when they should let a small blaze burn on the forest floor. A little fire destroys harmful insects and their eggs. It gets rid of dry leaves and fallen wood that could pile up and cause a huge fire later on.

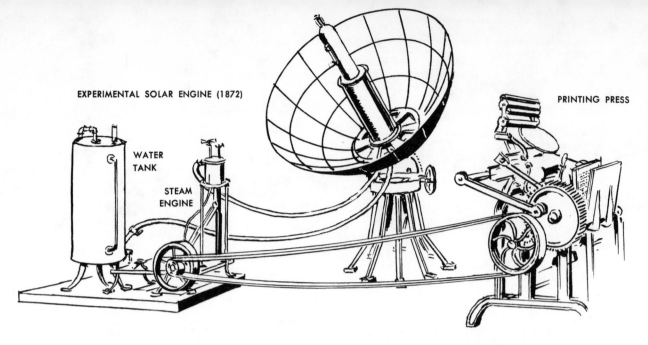

EXPERIMENTAL SOLAR ENGINE (1872)

WATER TANK

STEAM ENGINE

PRINTING PRESS

CAN WE GET ELECTRICITY FROM THE SUN?

WE ALREADY get electricity from the sun! But it comes to us in round-about ways. For example, we get it from power stations that are run by coal, and coal comes from plants that have been buried in the earth so long that they turned hard and black. Those plants were once alive. Like all other living things they depended on the sun for light and warmth in order to grow.

Some power stations are run by oil or natural gas. Oil and gas, like coal, come from living things that depended on the sun long ago.

We also get electricity from nuclear power stations. Perhaps this kind of power, too, comes from the sun. Some scientists think that the minerals that give us nuclear power were once part of the sun. In fact, they say, the whole earth was formed from material that broke away from the sun and began to circle around it.

All these ways of getting electricity have faults. The amount of coal and gas and oil under the earth is getting smaller every year. At the same time we need more and more power. The material that produces nuclear power is dangerous. An accident might release harmful radiation. Also, great heat is produced along with power, and the heat is hard to dispose of.

And so the world's scientists are looking for ways to get power directly from the sun. One idea is this: we may send satellites into orbit around the earth. They will collect some of the energy which the sun sends out.

116

Then the satellites will send the energy on to earth in much the same way that radio stations send out radio waves — without using wires or power lines. On earth, receiving stations will collect the energy, change it into electric current, and send it out over wires wherever it is needed.

The satellites for sun power would have to be enormous — more than a mile and a half wide, perhaps. The receivers would need to be even larger.

Perhaps all of this sounds like science fiction. But experts are sure they can do it when a real need for sun-power comes.

WHAT KEEPS A TRAIN ON THE TRACK?

IN THE old days train tracks were L-shaped, like the ones in the picture. The upright sides of the L's kept the wheels from slipping off.

Today the wheels themselves have a special shape. Each one has an inside rim called a flange. The main part of each wheel rests on the rail as it turns, and the flange keeps the wheel from sliding off the track.

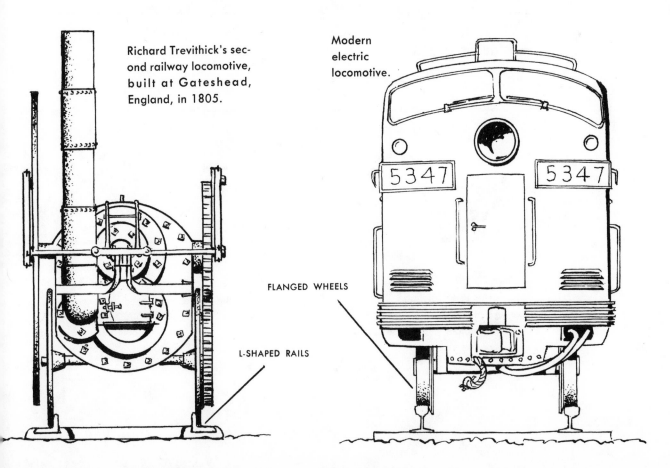

Richard Trevithick's second railway locomotive, built at Gateshead, England, in 1805.

Modern electric locomotive.

5347   5347

FLANGED WHEELS

L-SHAPED RAILS

WHY IS THE CITY WARMER THAN THE SUBURBS?

"TONIGHT," says the weatherman, "the temperature in Denver will be fifty degrees. Colder in the suburbs."

A city is almost always warmer than the country around it. Part of the extra heat comes from all the factories, furnaces, hot water tanks, truck and automobile engines in the city. There are fewer of these heat-makers in the suburbs and fewer still in the open country.

The city's concrete sidewalks and large brick buildings absorb a great deal of heat energy from the sun. They can store up much more heat in the daytime than soil and trees can. After the sun goes down they act like huge radiators keeping the city warm. In the suburbs these "radiators" are smaller and give off less heat at night.

The wind can carry away a great deal of heat from the spaces around low buildings and small houses. But tall factories and high-rise buildings slow the wind. And so the city's daytime heat is not blown away at night.

The country is often sunnier than the city where smoke or smog hang in the sky. Why doesn't the extra sunshine cause warmer temperatures? Smoke and smog actually form a sort of lid over the city, holding the heat in.

Look at the pictures and you will see still another reason for hot city weather.

Buildings and streets, fields and trees all reflect the warmth that radiates from the sun, just as a mirror reflects light. In the country much of the early-morning radiation is reflected into the open sky. But see what happens on a street lined with tall buildings. The radiation is reflected from one building to the pavement, then from pavement to another building, and finally into the open sky. Two buildings and the street absorb some heat! No wonder the city is warmer than the country.

WHY ARE CITIES SO BIG?

PEOPLE live together in groups because they need each other. They need to work together in factories or offices, and they also want to live with their families. This means that homes must be fairly close to the places of work.

Families need stores where they can buy things. Of course, the men and women who work in the stores must also have homes nearby. But not everybody can walk to the factory or office or store. Some drive to work, and they need filling stations and garages. Now the men who tend the gas pumps and repair the cars and mend the streets must also have homes. And they, too, need cars or buses or trains that will bring them to work.

All of this working and living and traveling brings more and more people together. Besides, more and more babies are born every year. When they are old enough for school, more and more teachers will be needed, and they, too, must travel or live nearby.

Nobody has yet found a way to keep cities from growing and growing and growing. Some are so big that they stretch out and meet other cities. You can't tell where one ends and another begins. Cities will keep on growing bigger so long as families grow — and so long as men and women go there to look for work.

Are cities getting too big? Some people think so. Others say that even the largest cities would be all right if good plans were made to keep them cleaner and quieter and easier to travel in. Some planners would like to have quiet little electric buses running quickly along the streets. No automobiles! Or perhaps moving sidewalks would be a better idea. Or what about helicopter buses that would bring you in from a home in the country and land you in front of the place where you work? (Many people who would like to live in the country can't stay there now because there is no work for them to do except in the city.)

City planners have many ideas like these to help improve cities which are still growing without any plan.

119

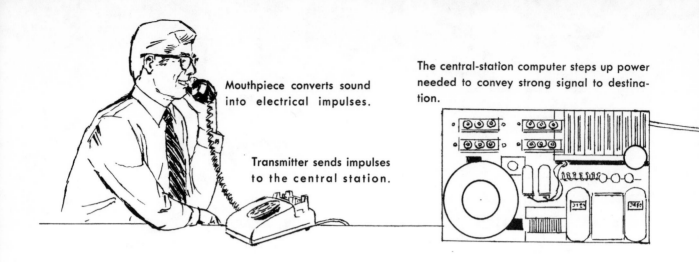

Mouthpiece converts sound into electrical impulses.

Transmitter sends impulses to the central station.

The central-station computer steps up power needed to convey strong signal to destination.

HOW DOES A LONG DISTANCE TELEPHONE CALL GET THERE SO FAST?

"HELLO!" you say into the phone.

"Hello!" comes the answer immediately from someone a thousand miles away. The two of you can talk just as well as if you were in the same room.

Of course, the sounds of your voices don't travel over the phone in the same way they travel across the room. In the air of the room your voice is carried by sound waves, but when you talk on the phone something else happens.

First the sound waves reach the telephone mouthpiece which is connected to a wire where a current of electricity can be turned on and off.

Next, inside the telephone, the sound waves are changed into electric signals. These electric signals travel along the wire to your friend's telephone far away.

Finally, in his telephone receiver the electric signals are changed into sound waves, exactly like the ones your voice made. Now when he talks, the sounds of his voice reach you in the same way.

All of this goes on very fast because electricity travels very fast. Electric current can go through wire on telephone poles at a speed of about 186,000 miles a second. That means it could zip all the way around the world seven times while you are saying "Hello!" — if there was a telephone line that long! Many long-distance calls travel through wires

120

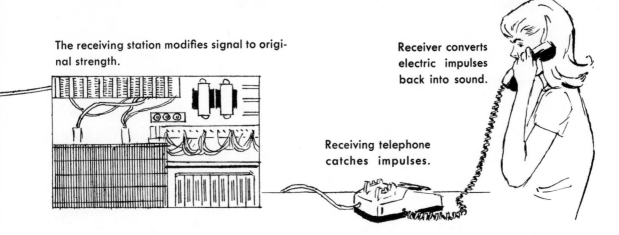

The receiving station modifies signal to original strength.

Receiver converts electric impulses back into sound.

Receiving telephone catches impulses.

bundled together in cables and buried under the earth. In these cables electric signals travel more slowly. They may go only about 93,000 miles in a second.

Some day long-distance calls will probably be handled in a different way. Sound signals from the telephone instrument will be changed into a special kind of signal that is carried by a beam of light called a laser light. Like electricity, light travels at 186,000 miles a second. The new phones will not make any difference in the way your voice sounds, but the beams will carry many more calls at a time than a cable does.

WHY DO SOME PEOPLE GET BALD?

USUALLY the people who are bald lose their hair as they grow older. A few at a time the hairs come out, and new ones do not grow in their place. Scientists cannot tell exactly why this happens to some people and not to others. They do know that a man is likely to be bald if some of his ancestors were bald. He was born with the kind of body and skin that do not make new hairs grow after he reaches a certain age. It is just as natural for him to lose his hair as it is for other men to keep theirs.

Women are less likely to have this kind of make-up than men are. Both men and women sometimes have illnesses, such as typhoid fever, that cause their hair to fall out. This kind of baldness does not usually last, and the hair soon grows in again.

WHY DO CHIGGER BITES MAKE YOU ITCH?

A CHIGGER is a tiny, red, eight-legged creature that belongs to a group called mites. (A tick is a very big mite.) Chiggers live in tall grass, mostly in the South, and as a rule they feed on insects. But if you come close enough, a chigger will leap onto you and bore its way quickly underneath your skin. It is so small that you don't feel it — at first.

Hidden under your skin, a chigger shoots out a kind of poison. Before long a poison-fighting substance in your body comes to the spot. This substance forms a small bump. By now you can feel something going on there. The poison has irritated the little nerve-endings in the skin. So you scratch. But scratching only spreads the poison, and the bump grows bigger. The larger the bump, the more you itch and scratch. Meantime, the bump protects the chigger while it feeds on you. At last, when it can eat no more, it crawls out and leaves you alone. But even after it is gone, you may keep on itching until the poison-fighters in your body have healed the wound that the chigger made.

Chiggers are sometimes called harvest mites because they bite men who harvest grain and hay. Actually, the mites prefer to eat insects, but they take what is closest. Since they are very sensitive to heat, they can always tell when a hot, hard-working human being is near.

WHAT IS THE "SOUTH 48"?

HERE IS a conversation that might have gone on between two people in Alaska before the year 1959:

    Question: "Where does your friend come from?"
    Answer: "The States."

Today the answer has to be different. Why? Because Alaska itself is now in the United States. Before 1959 it was not a state. It was a territory. Today an Alaskan would say: "My friend comes from the South 48." This means that his friend lives in one of the 48 states south of the Canadian border.

During the blizzard of 1888 some people were able to find their way back to the house from the barn by following a fence. Others were lost in the blinding swirl and froze, sometimes within yards of their house.

WHAT IS A BLIZZARD?

A SNOWSTORM, plus a very strong and very cold wind — that is what makes a blizzard. A blizzard is worse than an ordinary storm because the wind sweeps snow from some places and heaps it up in other places. Snowdrifts may cover doors and windows so that people can't leave their houses. Automobiles get stuck in drifts.

In the famous blizzard of 1888 fierce winds produced monstrous drifts, some of them sixty feet deep. Snow buried whole trains on the tracks, and passengers had to stay in the railroad cars for days before snowplows finally dug the trains out. That probably wouldn't happen today, because helicopters can land on the snow and rescue people as soon as a blizzard dies down.

HOW DOES A TAPE RECORDER WORK?

THE TAPE for a tape recorder looks like a roll of dirty plastic ribbon. And so it is. The thin plastic tape has been dusted with tiny particles of iron.

On a new roll of tape, the bits of iron lie helter-skelter, fixed to the surface of the plastic. But if a magnet comes near the tape, the bits of iron will move. You can't see them moving, because they are very tiny, but they really do change position. The magnet makes them line up and form a pattern, while at the same time they stay fixed to the tape.

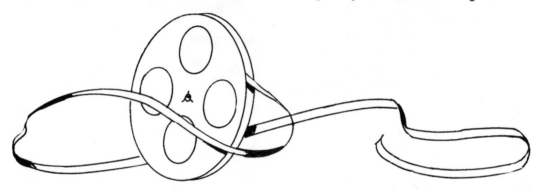

Inside a tape recorder there is a special kind of magnet that works by electricity. There is also a little motor that pulls the tape past the magnet. And there is a plug which connects the magnet to a microphone.

To make a tape recording of your voice, you plug in the microphone. Next you push a button, and the tape begins to roll past the magnet. Then you talk into the microphone. As you talk, your voice makes a pattern of sound. The microphone changes this sound pattern to a pattern in the electric current that goes to the magnet. Magnetism then arranges the iron particles on the tape into patterns that correspond to the sound-patterns of your voice.

As long as the tape keeps rolling past the magnet, and as long as sounds reach the microphone, the iron particles will keep on being arranged in patterns. And after they have been arranged, they stay in place, as long as an electric magnet does not rearrange them. Equally important, the particles themselves have become magnetic.

124

To hear what you have recorded on the tape, you first push a button which makes the motor roll the tape back to the beginning. Then you switch off the microphone and switch on a loudspeaker which is inside the recorder box. The loudspeaker does the opposite of what the microphone does. It changes electrical patterns into sound patterns. When the tape rolls forward again, the magnetized iron particles make a pattern in the electric current flowing through a wire to the loudspeaker. The loudspeaker changes this pattern into a pattern of sound — the same sound-pattern that your voice made when you first spoke into the microphone.

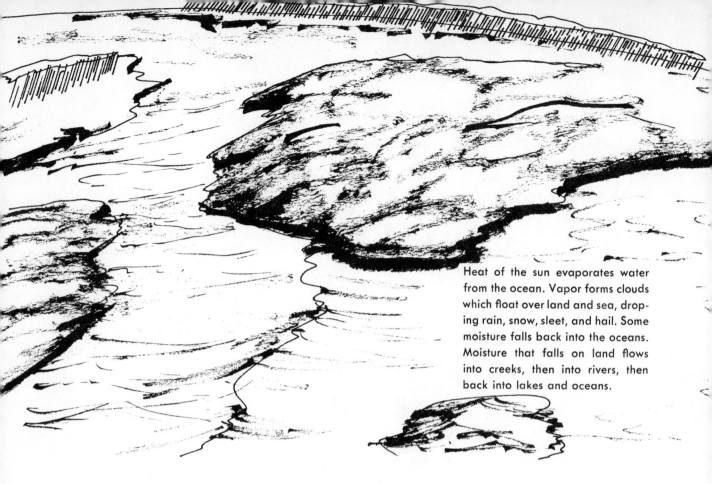

Heat of the sun evaporates water from the ocean. Vapor forms clouds which float over land and sea, dropping rain, snow, sleet, and hail. Some moisture falls back into the oceans. Moisture that falls on land flows into creeks, then into rivers, then back into lakes and oceans.

WHY DOESN'T THE OCEAN DRY UP?

IN SOME years, much less rain falls near your home than in other years. If several years go by with little rain, people say there is a drought. Streams get smaller. Lakes and reservoirs are almost dry. Cities may have a water shortage. But, if you live near the seashore, you can see that the drought doesn't seem to make the ocean any smaller!

To see why, remember that rain clouds don't ever form at exactly the same place and time every year. Winds blow differently each year. The temperature is different. When you have a dry year, many heavy rain clouds may form in a neighboring place. Or there may be enormous rainstorms over the ocean where people don't see them.

Of course, clouds are formed in the first place when water evaporates from the ocean and from lakes and streams and plants and people. Like a slow wheel turning, over a long period of time, water circulates from ocean to sky and back again.

126

WHAT IS A "TALKING BOOK"?

"Talking Books" are really long-playing phonograph records. They are made especially for people who cannot see but can listen to the records instead of reading the printed words. Anyone who needs a Talking Book can borrow the record from the Library of Congress in Washington, D.C. The Library sends the records by mail in special boxes, and the borrower returns them in the same boxes which don't need to have any postage stamps. There are Talking Books of many kinds for both children and adults.

Blind people can also read books with their fingers! These books are printed in a special kind of writing called Braille. The Braille alphabet is made up of tiny round bumps stamped into the paper. One bump stands for the letter A. Add another under it and you have B. To make C, you put the second dot beside the first, not under it. With various arrangements of the bumps, the whole alphabet can be made. Anyone who learns and remembers the arrangements can touch the bumps with his fingertips and spell out words written in Braille.

The man who invented this kind of writing, Louis Braille, had a good reason for doing so. He taught in a school for blind people — and he himself was blind.

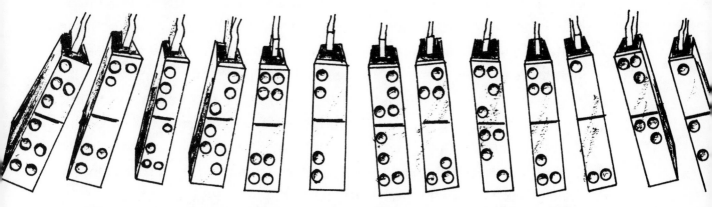

Even if you don't know the Braille alphabet, you can write letters to blind people, using a special typewriter. You strike regular typewriter keys, almost as if you were writing an ordinary letter. The typewriter arms jump up and hit the paper. But the type at the end of each arm is not ordinary type. It is Braille type, made with little round knobs. When the knobs strike the paper, they make dents in it. Turn the paper over, and the dents form the raised bumps which a blind person can read with his fingers.

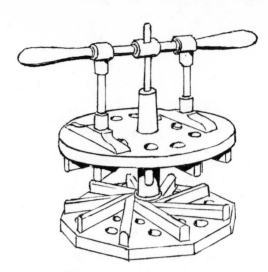

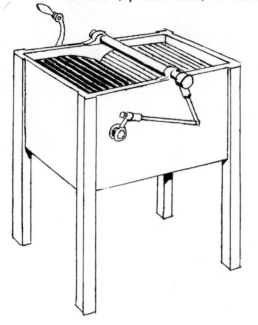

This machine was meant to be used in an ordinary tub. The upper part was turned back and forth, and up and down. Cleats on the lower disc swirled the clothes in the water.

HOW DOES A WASHING MACHINE GET CLOTHES CLEAN?

A WASHING MACHINE does just about what women learned to do by hand in very ancient times. At first they simply swished dirty clothes around in water. The swishing loosened some dirt, and water carried it away. Then about five thousand years ago someone in the land of Sumer invented soap. The soap loosened and carried away more dirt than plain water did. Unfortunately the men of Sumer got into wars with neighbors. People were killed. Their cities were destroyed and after a while no one remembered how to make soap. Later, women in other countries found that a certain kind of salt mixed with wash water helped to take out dirt. The detergents we put into washing machines are something like that salt.

Years passed, and finally soap was invented all over again. In some places women learned a special trick that made washing easier. They dipped each piece of clothing in a stream, soaped it and laid it on a flat

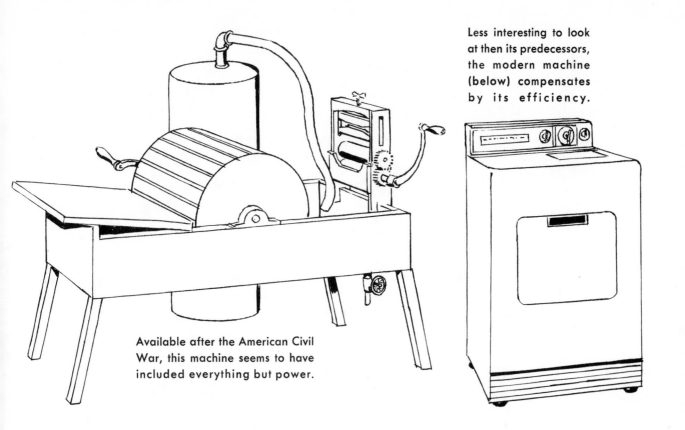

Available after the American Civil War, this machine seems to have included everything but power.

rock. Then they smacked it hard with a large wooden paddle. The paddle jarred the dirt loose from the cloth, and after that the soap and water carried it away.

At last men invented electric motors that turned machinery, and in 1937 the first automatic washing machine was built. Now there are many different kinds. One kind is made with a movable arm in the middle of a tub. The motor moves the arm, and it swishes clothes back and forth through the water. Another kind of machine bounces clothes up and down in the water. Still another has a revolving tub that tumbles the clothes, carrying them up and over and down again. Sometimes they fall against the bottom of the tub with a smack, and that helps to loosen dirt, just as the old-fashioned wooden paddle did.

Most machines have a way of spinning water out of the clothes when the washing is finished. As the tub whirls around, clothes and water are forced outward against the tub's side. The dirty water flies off through small holes in the tub, while the clean clothes stay inside.

WHAT ARE CIVIL RIGHTS?

IN SOME COUNTRIES there are laws saying that ordinary citizens must be allowed to do certain things. The word for citizens in the old Latin language was *civilis*. Then Englishmen borrowed the word long ago, and that is why we say *civil* rights when we talk about the things a person can do just because he is a citizen.

A citizen of the United States has the right to vote — in some places after he is 21 years old, in other places after he is 18. This is a civil right that belongs to men and women alike, no matter what their religion is or where their ancestors came from.

In the United States a law says that all children have equal rights to get an education. No school is supposed to keep any child out because of the color of his skin.

Restaurants are supposed to allow anyone to buy a meal.

Employers aren't supposed to refuse to hire a citizen just because she is a woman.

People who work have the right to join a union.

Citizens who wanted and needed all these rights had to try for a long time before they got laws which guaranteed them. But laws are not always obeyed. Employers sometimes find ways not to hire women who could do certain jobs as well as men. Many black people still have a hard time voting, and many black children can't go to schools with white children. Still people keep trying to see that the laws are obeyed. That is why there is so much talk about civil rights.

Influential barons and clergy met King John of England at Runnymede in June, 1215, and forced him to sign the Magna Carta, a charter of liberties.

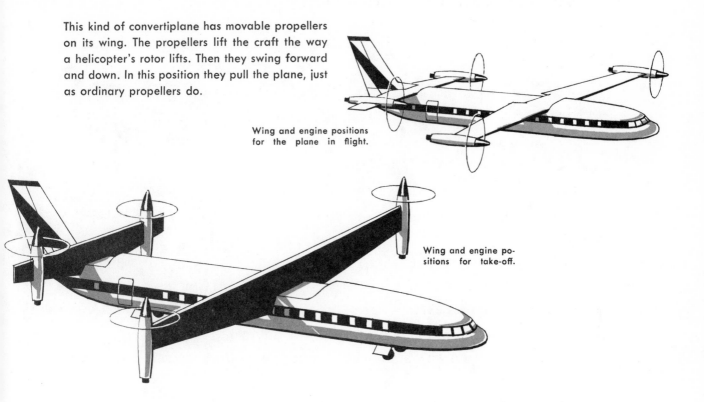

This kind of convertiplane has movable propellers on its wing. The propellers lift the craft the way a helicopter's rotor lifts. Then they swing forward and down. In this position they pull the plane, just as ordinary propellers do.

Wing and engine positions for the plane in flight.

Wing and engine positions for take-off.

WHAT IS A CONVERTIPLANE?

AN ORDINARY airplane must run along the ground getting up speed before it can take off. As a rule, the bigger the plane, the longer the runway it needs. And the longer the runways, the larger the airports must be. There are already so many huge planes landing on long runways near cities that some people think it would be dangerous to build any more large airports.

Why not use helicopters? They can land and take off in a much smaller space than a plane. The trouble is that a helicopter cannot travel so fast after it gets into the air, and many people do not want to travel slowly.

The perfect aircraft, then, would be as big and fast as an airplane but able to go almost straight up and down like a helicopter. Many airplane manufacturers have already built experimental models of a machine that the pilot can change from helicopter to airplane and back to helicopter. They call it a convertiplane because the pilot can convert it from one kind of flight to another whenever he needs to.

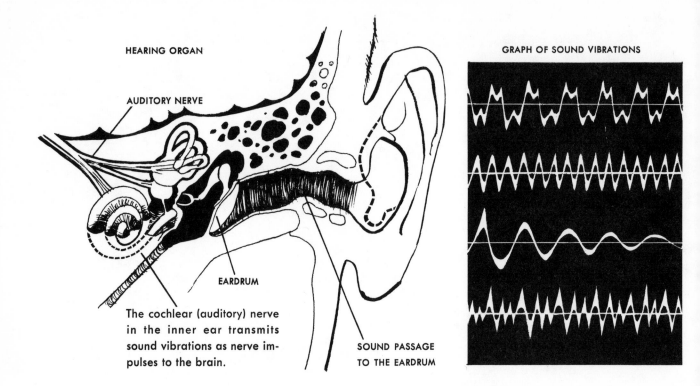

HEARING ORGAN

AUDITORY NERVE

EARDRUM

The cochlear (auditory) nerve in the inner ear transmits sound vibrations as nerve impulses to the brain.

SOUND PASSAGE TO THE EARDRUM

GRAPH OF SOUND VIBRATIONS

WHY ARE SOME NOISES SOFT AND SOME LOUD?

STRETCH a rubber band between the thumb and first finger of one hand, then pluck it gently. You can feel it vibrating, moving quickly in and out, tapping your skin. At the same time the rubber band bumps against the millions of tiny invisible particles of air all around it. The particles, called molecules, now begin to vibrate. They bump into neighboring molecules, and these, too, vibrate. The bumping and vibrating go on and on, forming little waves in the air. Finally the waves travel into your ear and air molecules tap against a thin wall of skin — the eardrum. It is a gentle tapping. The eardrum moves only a little way in and out. And a signal goes to your brain: "Soft noise."

Now suppose you pluck the rubber band harder. It taps more sharply against your hand. It also hits the air molecules harder. Stronger sound waves reach your eardrum, and the signal goes to your brain: "Louder noise."

Very strong sound waves will tap your eardrums very hard, and so you say: "Very loud noise!"

You hear a loud noise when an alarm-clock bell rings close to your ear. But the sound is very soft if the same bell rings in a distant part of the house. How can that be? The answer is that sound waves get weaker as they travel.

Would you believe that a noise could be loud enough for you to hear 3,000 miles away? That was what happened many years ago when a volcano erupted on an island called Krakatoa off the southern coast of Asia. The volcano exploded suddenly. A whole mountain blew up all at once and caused sound waves so strong that people in far-off Japan heard the noise. Even though sound travels fast (about 770 miles an hour), it was nearly four hours before the Japanese people heard the explosion.

WHAT IS A DECIBEL?

DECIBEL is a word that scientists use when they talk about the loudness of sounds. A decibel is a unit of measurement — just as an inch is a unit on a ruler. Inches tell you how long things are. Decibels tell you how strong sound waves are.

The "ruler" for sounds is called the decibel scale. What is the softest noise it can measure? A butterfly landing? That would be almost zero on the decibel scale. A little farther above zero on the scale you can hear yourself breathing. The noise level in a house with the TV tuned rather low is about 50 on the scale — unless the program happens to be funny. Giggles add decibels. In an automobile factory the noise level goes up to 95 or more. At about 130 on the decibel scale sounds make your ears hurt.

The study of sound interested a young man named Alexander Graham Bell about a hundred years ago. Bell was a teacher in a school for deaf children, and he tried to understand exactly how voices work. Later the things he learned about sounds helped him to invent the telephone. Still later, when scientists found a way to measure the loudness of sounds, they needed a new word for their unit of measurement. So they invented the name decibel in honor of Alexander Bell.

HOW DOES A JACKHAMMER WORK?

LONG AGO men discovered how to make holes in rock. First they shaped a piece of hard metal so that it had a sharp point. This they called a drill. Then, hitting the drill with a heavy hammer, they could knock off bits of rock, a few at a time, until at last they had worn away a hole. Men still use this same method when they want to cut a hole in the pavement or break up a cement sidewalk. But the hammer and the drill are now combined into one powerful tool called a jackhammer. It is also called an air drill because air instead of muscle moves the hammer up and down.

First, a lot of air has to be squeezed into a tank. This compressed air can then be let out through a hose. When it comes out, it gives a very hard push. It can push hard enough to make the hammer strike the drill so that it cuts into asphalt or cement.

The hammer, which moves up and down inside the air-drill tool, does not look like an ordinary hammer. It looks more like a one-legged stool, and it is called a piston. When air pushes against the top of the

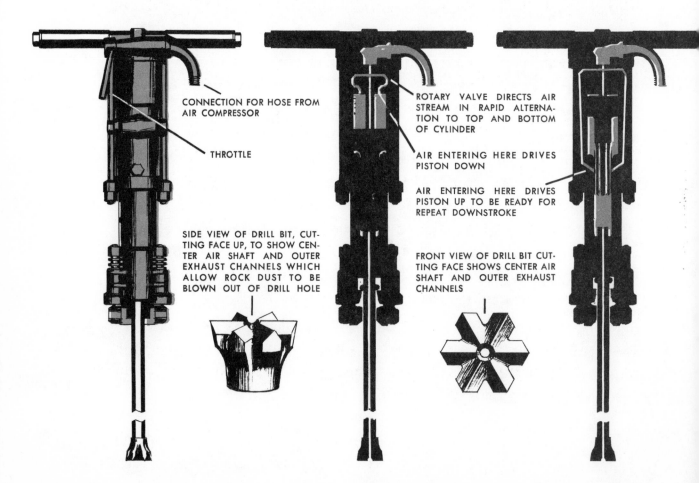

CONNECTION FOR HOSE FROM AIR COMPRESSOR

THROTTLE

SIDE VIEW OF DRILL BIT, CUTTING FACE UP, TO SHOW CENTER AIR SHAFT AND OUTER EXHAUST CHANNELS WHICH ALLOW ROCK DUST TO BE BLOWN OUT OF DRILL HOLE

ROTARY VALVE DIRECTS AIR STREAM IN RAPID ALTERNATION TO TOP AND BOTTOM OF CYLINDER

AIR ENTERING HERE DRIVES PISTON DOWN

AIR ENTERING HERE DRIVES PISTON UP TO BE READY FOR REPEAT DOWNSTROKE

FRONT VIEW OF DRILL BIT CUTTING FACE SHOWS CENTER AIR SHAFT AND OUTER EXHAUST CHANNELS piston, the piston goes down, and the leg hits the top end of the drill. This drives the point of the drill against the asphalt. At that moment a little gate closes above the piston. This gate, called a valve, stops the compressed air from coming in. At the same time another valve opens underneath the piston. Compressed air rushes in there and shoves the piston up. Then this valve closes, the other one opens, and air shoots against the top of the piston again. Down it goes with a bang.

Compressed air keeps on driving the piston up and down very fast. And so the drill point swiftly breaks its way into asphalt or concrete.

WHY DON'T BIRDS' FEET FREEZE IN WINTER?

BIRDS with bare feet and legs can live outdoors in freezing weather. If you tried to do that, you would be very uncomfortable. Your toes might even get frostbitten. One reason is that your body's heating system is different from a bird's. You have a special temperature regulator at the base of your brain. When you go out into the cold, this part of the brain sends messages to the muscles which control tiny blood vessels just beneath the skin. The muscles tighten up, and less of your warm blood now flows through the vessels. So your skin becomes cooler. Your feet and hands feel cold unless they are covered. At the same time your heart and other important organs inside your body stay warm because heat is not lost through the skin.

Many birds do not have this kind of heat regulation. The blood vessels in their skin do not grow smaller as soon as the outside world gets cold. Also their bodies have a higher temperature than yours. And so enough heat reaches a bird's feet to keep them from freezing.

Where does the heat come from? Both your body and the bird's must use food to produce warmth. Some birds have such warm bodies that they must eat a great deal of food. If you ate like that kind of bird you would need at least 25 pounds of food at every meal!

Sometimes hens lay eggs with very thick shells. That usually means they have been frightened or upset by a change in the world around them. Did changes in the world upset egg-laying dinosaurs millions of years ago? Scientists wonder. They have found fossil dinosaur eggs that have six or seven layers of shell. The eggs were laid at just about the time when dinosaurs began to die out. Perhaps a change in the earth's temperature or moisture bothered dinosaurs so much that they laid eggs with shells too thick for baby dinosaurs to break. When fewer and fewer eggs hatched, the huge animals gradually died out.

WHAT ARE EGGSHELLS MADE OF?

AN EGGSHELL is made of a substance called calcium carbonate. Another name for it is lime. Seashells are made of lime, too. Drinking water often contains some of it. So do many plants. So do bones and limestone rocks — and of course the body of the hen that lays the eggs.

The yellow part — the yolk — of an egg is made first. It forms in an organ called the ovary. The yolk then begins to slide through a tube where the other parts are added. As it moves along the tube it is covered with a large blob of egg white. Next, a thin, tough covering called a membrane forms around the white, and now the egg is ready for the shell. It moves on to a part of the egg-tube called the shell gland. There a thin coat of lime is slowly deposited all over the membrane. The lime hardens, and the egg is pushed out of the tube.

Lime for eggshells comes from the food that chickens eat. They get some of it in wheat and corn and other grains, some in water. Just to make sure they have enough, farmers usually mix ground-up seashells or limestone with the food.

136

ARE REINDEER THE SAME AS CARIBOU?

THESE TWO kinds of animal are close relatives. They look very much alike, and their homes are in the cold parts of the world near the Arctic Ocean. Reindeer live in Europe and Asia. Caribou live in North America.

Thousands of years ago men in Siberia began to tame the reindeer and kept them in herds. The Eskimos in North America never tried to tame the caribou, but they did hunt them — and still do. Every year great numbers of these fast-moving animals travel back and forth across parts of Alaska and Canada.

Will caribou still migrate from place to place if roads and oil pipelines cross their paths? Scientists are not sure. Modern inventions may interfere with the habits of the animals and also with the plants they eat. The ecology of Alaska may be greatly changed. And so scientists believe that it would be a good idea to bring in new things very slowly. That will give them a chance to test each one. Perhaps they can make plans so that changes do as little harm as possible.

REINDEER

CARIBOU

WHAT IS TUNDRA?

THE STORY of the word tundra starts with people called Lapps who live along the cold northern edges of Europe and Asia. The land there is almost level, and in summer, when the ground thaws, it turns swampy. To describe their country the Lapps used a two-part word *tun-tur*, which means *bog-flat land*.

Long ago the Lapps taught the word *tun-tur* to their neighbors, the Russians. Then English-speaking people learned it from the Russians. But somewhere along the line *tun-tur* came to be pronounced tundra.

There is tundra all around the Arctic Ocean, in Alaska and Canada as well as Europe and Asia. On this arctic prairie land, little plants grow so thick that they feel like cushions underfoot. The only trees are tiny willows, no taller than your little finger. Big trees cannot live on soil that gives them moisture for just two summer months. But grasses sprout quickly on the tundra, and millions of tiny bright flowers bloom. In places

you can find a strange kind of plant called lichen. A lichen is really two plants which form a partnership, each helping the other to grow. One partner belongs to a group of plants called algae. (Some seaweeds are also algae.) The other partner is a fungus. (A mushroom is also a fungus.) These two plants cling side by side to bits of soil or even to bare rocks where nothing else can grow.

All of the tundra's plants resist the long, icy winters. Cold does not harm them. But man does. This was a great surprise to people who moved into Alaska with machinery to drill oil wells and build roads and pipelines. A truck or tractor leaves a path of ruined land when it makes just one trip across the tundra, and it will take years for the plants to cover the ground again, because they grow very slowly. When arctic plant life is killed, other damage may be done to the soil and to animal life. Is it really a good idea to go ahead with building projects in Alaska? Or should men wait until scientists have had time to figure out just what kind of building will do the least harm?

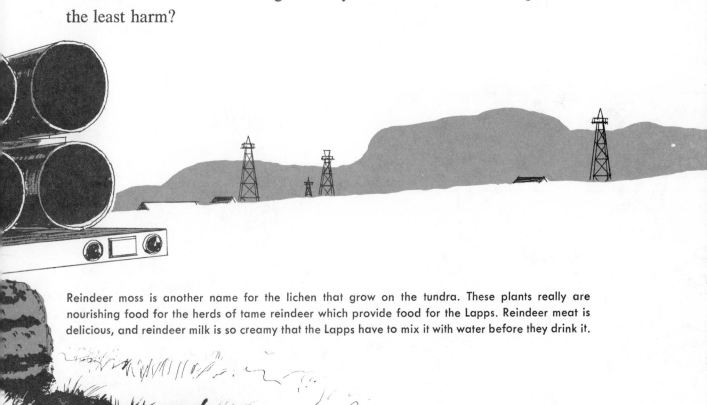

Reindeer moss is another name for the lichen that grow on the tundra. These plants really are nourishing food for the herds of tame reindeer which provide food for the Lapps. Reindeer meat is delicious, and reindeer milk is so creamy that the Lapps have to mix it with water before they drink it.

WHAT IS A CURFEW?

SOMETIMES the police in a city make a rule that people must stay in their houses, off the streets, after a certain hour at night. This rule is called a curfew.

Originally curfew meant *cover-the-fire*. The expression began more than a thousand years ago in Europe. In those days each house had a big open fireplace for cooking and heating. Many houses were built of wood with roofs of bundled straw. Such a building could easily burn down if a spark flew out of the fireplace or up the chimney and onto the straw roof.

When one house burned, a whole city might go up in flames, because there were no fire engines, and water had to be brought from wells or streams by hand. So a safety law required people to cover their fires with ashes before they went to bed at night. A bell rang to warn that it was cover-fire time. Anyone who was still on the street had to go indoors and take care of the fire when the curfew bell rang.

Most cities today have no regular curfew law. In some places teen-agers must be at home before a curfew time which the city officials decide on. Sometimes, if there is trouble between two groups of people, the police make a curfew rule that keeps everybody indoors at night. Like the ancient cover-fire bell, the curfew says "Cool it."

NORWEGIAN VILLAGE HOUSE, A.D. 1000

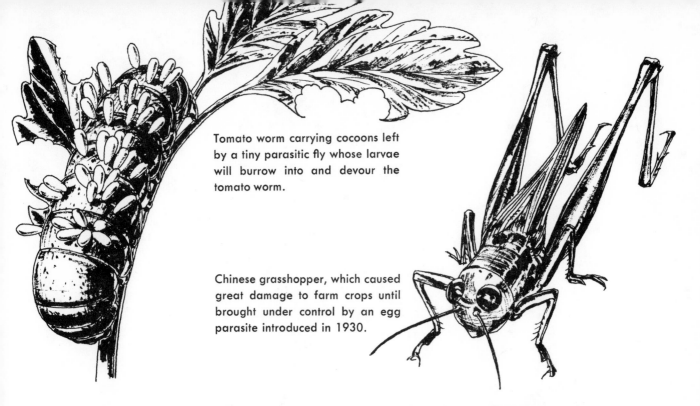

Tomato worm carrying cocoons left by a tiny parasitic fly whose larvae will burrow into and devour the tomato worm.

Chinese grasshopper, which caused great damage to farm crops until brought under control by an egg parasite introduced in 1930.

IS THERE A SAFE WAY TO KILL INSECT PESTS?

PEOPLE once thought it was safe to kill pests with chemical poisons. Now scientists are not sure. They are afraid that DDT and other chemicals may be harmful to human beings. So they have looked for other ways to get rid of insects. They have already found out how to keep some kinds of flies from laying eggs that will hatch.

How about catching insects in traps? That might work if we could find the right bait. Experimenters know that some male moths are attracted by a special scent which the female makes in her body. If special scents can be made in factories, they might be good bait for traps. Males caught in the traps could not fertilize any eggs. Fewer eggs would then hatch. The next year there would be fewer insects for the traps to catch, and finally perhaps none at all.

Scientists have also discovered that they can use an insect's own natural enemies. There are certain germs that only attack cabbage worms. Another kind of germ kills grasshoppers but nothing else. Just to make sure these germs are safe for people, doctors have swallowed big doses of them. Nothing happened. Still, scientists must go on testing such things carefully. But someday, they hope, they may be able to control all the worst pests in ways that do not harm people or spoil the world we live in.

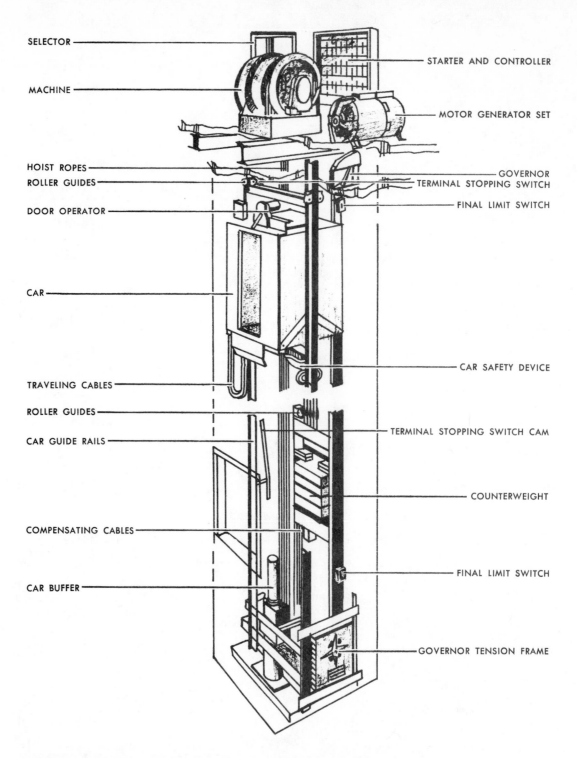

SELECTOR

MACHINE

HOIST ROPES

ROLLER GUIDES

DOOR OPERATOR

CAR

TRAVELING CABLES

ROLLER GUIDES

CAR GUIDE RAILS

COMPENSATING CABLES

CAR BUFFER

STARTER AND CONTROLLER

MOTOR GENERATOR SET

GOVERNOR
TERMINAL STOPPING SWITCH

FINAL LIMIT SWITCH

CAR SAFETY DEVICE

TERMINAL STOPPING SWITCH CAM

COUNTERWEIGHT

FINAL LIMIT SWITCH

GOVERNOR TENSION FRAME

HOW DOES AN ELEVATOR WORK?

AN ELEVATOR full of people is very heavy. The machinery that lifts it must be very strong, but inventors have made the lifting job easier than you might think. Look at the diagram and you will see how.

At the top of the building is an electric motor. It turns a wheel that has a groove around its rim, and in the groove fits the steel rope that hauls the elevator car up and down. This wheel, and another one at the bottom of the building, help to make the car glide smoothly along.

Another helper is a heavy block of metal called the counterweight. The weight pulls down on the cable while the motor is pulling the elevator up. Going down, the elevator which is heavier than the counterweight does most of the work of raising the weight into position so it can help the electric motor again next time.

Dozens of electric switches connect the motor with the different parts of the whole elevator system. Switches control the opening and closing of the door, work the brakes that slow the car, and operate safety devices that stop it in case anything goes wrong.

HOW DOES AN ELEVATOR KNOW WHEN TO STOP?

THE BUTTONS inside an elevator work switches outside it. These switches are something like the ones that turn electricity on and off in your house. They are connected with the electric motor that sends the elevator car up and down. When the car reaches the top floor of a building, a special switch automatically signals the motor to stop pulling.

In a tall building people on twenty different floors may be pushing buttons at about the same time. Some want to go up. Some want to go down. The car stops for people at all the right floors going up, and then for those who pushed the down buttons. It seems to remember what to do. Of course an elevator doesn't have a brain that keeps track of all the signals. Instead it is connected to a computer — a machine that has a kind of mechanical memory. The computer itself is connected to the motor that starts and stops the elevator car. The electric signals travel very fast, and so the car can answer quickly when people push the buttons.

HOW FAST DOES AN ELEVATOR GO?

ELEVATORS in tall buildings often travel at a speed of 1500 feet a minute. That is a little more than 17 miles an hour.

When you are riding in an automobile, 17 miles an hour seems rather slow. But in an elevator it seems very fast, partly because you aren't used to the feeling of going up or down so quickly. Many elevators could be made to move at even higher speeds. But passengers would probably complain!

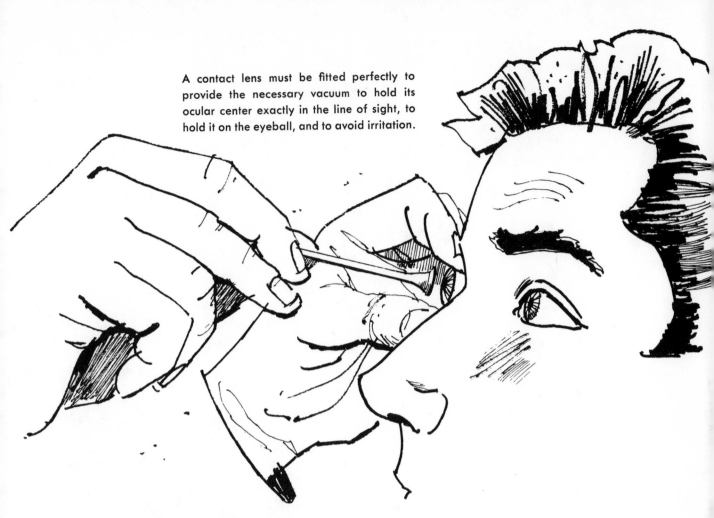

A contact lens must be fitted perfectly to provide the necessary vacuum to hold its ocular center exactly in the line of sight, to hold it on the eyeball, and to avoid irritation.

WHAT ARE CONTACT LENSES?

IN THE MIDDLE of each of your eyes is a small, round black spot. This is really an opening, like a round window, which lets light enter your eye so that you can see. In the opening is a tiny cover, as clear as glass. This cover is called the lens of the eye.

Some people have lenses in their eyes that work perfectly. They can see things far away or close by or in between. Other people have trouble seeing well. Often the lenses inside their eyes need help. So they wear glasses, which are extra lenses in frames outside their eyes.

Most of the helping lenses are made of glass. That is why we call them glasses. But a lens can also be made of plastic. A plastic lens can be very small. In fact it can be so small that it doesn't have to be worn outside the eye. It can be placed right on the eyeball — in contact with it. That is why it is called a contact lens.

145

This escalator has an incline of 30 degrees. Its steps move at a speed of 90 feet per minute and will carry eight thousand passengers per hour. The end-view cross section of two stairways mounted side by side shows how the wheels of each step ride on four separate tracks, a pair for the front of each step and a pair for the rear.

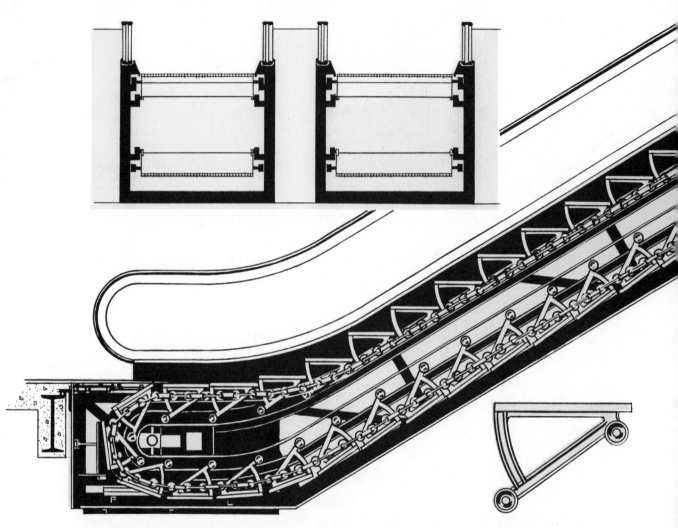

A single step, viewed from the end on the rising side, shows the articulated mounting of two wheels. The comb tread meshes with the comb at the landing, easing the transfer of passengers from the moving vehicle to a stationary surface.

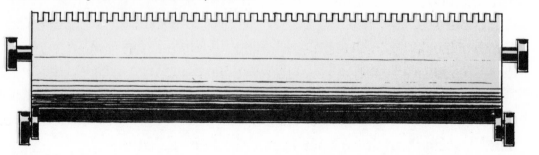

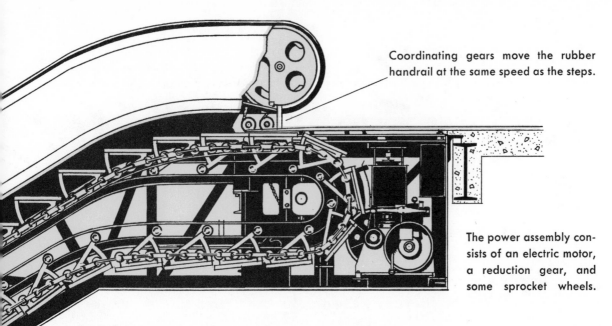

Coordinating gears move the rubber handrail at the same speed as the steps.

The power assembly consists of an electric motor, a reduction gear, and some sprocket wheels.

HOW DOES AN ESCALATOR WORK?

AN ESCALATOR is a moving stairway that can carry people up or down from one floor of a building to another. The stair-steps are attached to chains, somewhat like bicycle chains. On a bicycle the pedals turn a spikey-looking disc called a sprocket. The sprocket's little spikes catch the chain and make it move. On the escalator electric motors turn huge sprockets which make the chains move, and the chains pull the steps either up or down.

Each step is built like a little flatcar. The flat top of the car is the part you stand on. Each step rests on four wheels that run smoothly on tracks as the chain pulls the car along.

Now suppose the escalator is carrying you up from the first to the second story of a building. The wheels roll uphill on their tracks, but they are arranged in a very clever way so that the step you stand on stays level as it goes up the sloping track. Soon the top of your step is even with the floor of the second story, and you can walk right off.

Your step now rolls on under the floor, pulled by the chains. Then like the bicycle chain, the escalator chains continue their round trip, down, then up and over the top again in an endless circle.

It takes you longer to ride upstairs on an escalator than in an elevator. But even though it goes slower than an elevator, an escalator can carry ten times as many people an hour from one floor to another.

147

WHY DO SOME PEOPLE GET DIVORCED?

SOMETIMES you find a friend you will like all your life. But it can also happen that you and a friend become interested in very different things. The two of you have less and less to talk about and to agree on. Your friendship is not as strong as it used to be. As friendship for one person fades, friendship for someone else may grow stronger. That's the way it is with boys and girls. The same thing may happen to adults.

Sometimes a husband and wife get different interests and different friends. They don't enjoy being together. In fact, they would rather not be together at all. There may be only one thing they really agree on — both of them love their children.

When a husband and wife feel this way, they may decide that they don't want to stay married. One or both of them talk to a person called a judge, who has the job of listening to this kind of problem. He thinks first about the children and what will be best for them. Then, if he believes everybody will be happier, he will agree that the husband and wife can end their marriage. He says they may have a divorce. This means that the husband and wife do not have to live together any longer.

In the United States and many other countries, there are laws about divorce. A divorced man may marry another wife. A divorced woman may marry another husband. Or they may stay unmarried. But the officials of some churches do not always agree with these laws. People who belong to these churches do not, as a rule, become divorced.

Children often wish their parents would not be divorced. Every child wants both a mother and a father to love him. But mothers and fathers want love, too, and it is sometimes hard for everybody to get all the love he needs and deserves.

DO WET FEET MAKE YOU CATCH COLD?

SCIENTISTS, who wanted to know the answer to that question, asked some men to help with an experiment. None of the men had a cold when the experiment started. Some of them deliberately got wet and chilly. But they did not catch cold any more often than others who stayed dry and warm!

Another part of the experiment showed that people *do* catch cold most often when they are exposed to the germs that cause colds. These germs are easily scattered around a room by coughs and sneezes and sniffles. So, if you get wet feet and come into a house where nobody is sniffling, you yourself will probably escape without sniffles. But if you come with wet feet into a house where someone has a cold, and if his germs give you a cold — the wet feet will probably be blamed.

ARE PEOPLE MACHINES?

WHEN YOU ask questions about the human body, the answers may make you think that people are machines: "Your heart is a kind of pump." Or "Nerves are tiny threads that carry messages from different parts of the body to the brain." Or "A computer is a mechanical brain."

People are really very different from machines. One important difference is this: men build machines, but no machine ever built a human being!

A computer is a machine that can do a million arithmetic problems a minute. Even a genius can't work that fast. Still, it was the human brain that discovered how to make the computer. And the best computer in the world could not put together a living girl or boy.

WHAT IS DDT?

WHEN A CHEMICAL has a very long name, scientists may decide to shorten it. For example, there is dichloro-diphenyl-trichloro-ethane. Try spelling it and you'll see why almost everybody now calls it DDT. The letters are the first three initials in that four-part word.

The scientist who gave DDT its 31-letter name wasn't trying to show off. The different parts of his word tell other scientists exactly what the substance is made of. You do the same thing when you say chocolate-marshmallow-nut sundae.

At first DDT seemed like a wonderful discovery. It killed flies and mosquitoes and other insect pests. But it did not seem to harm either human beings or animals. And so it was mixed into sprays and powders and put to work all over the world. Then came the bad news: DDT really could do harm. It killed some of the birds that ate the poisoned insects. It made some eggshells so thin that they broke when mother birds sat on them in their nests. When DDT was sprayed on plants, cows ate it along with their food. The cows didn't get sick, but DDT appeared in their milk, and of course people drank the milk. Fish, too, swallowed DDT that the

After aerial dusting of marsh for pest control, ecologists take samples of insect and marine life to be examined in the laboratory for good and bad effects of the chemical that was used.

rain washed away from fields where it had been sprayed, and then people ate the fish.

At last scientists began to worry. A little DDT didn't bother most human beings, but doctors were afraid there would soon be too much of it in the world. Then it might cause a great deal of sickness. Wasn't there some way to have the good effects of the chemical but avoid the bad? Experimenters did find a way to keep DDT out of milk. They mixed charcoal with the cows' food. The charcoal wasn't digested. It simply absorbed the DDT and then went on out of the cows' bodies along with other wastes.

Perhaps that would solve the milk problem. But what about other foods? You couldn't feed charcoal to all the fish in the sea! Scientists decided to invent a new chemical to mix with DDT. The new chemical would not harm living things. It would allow DDT to kill insects, but immediately afterward it would change the DDT into something different and safe.

This and other ideas had to be tested. Meantime it seemed wise to stop spreading the poison. In some places DDT could be used only to kill such pests as the mosquitoes which carry disease germs. In other places sprays made with DDT were no longer used at all.

WHY DO CATS HAVE SHARP CLAWS?

A CAT'S CLAWS developed in ancient times, when it had to hunt for all its food. The hungry cat would lie very still, waiting for a mouse or a bird to come close. Then suddenly it would pounce. Its weight knocked its prey off balance, and the sharp, hooked claws held tight to fur or feathers.

Everything about a cat is fitted for a special kind of hunting. Its legs are not very long, but the muscles are powerful. So it can leap quickly and strike hard. The claws move out when they are needed, but are pulled back and protected in little sheaths most of the time. So they stay sharp.

Sometimes a cat stands on its hind legs and rakes its claws along the side of a chair or the bark of a tree. It seems to be sharpening the claws. More likely it is just exercising the muscles in its legs and feet.

A dog's claws are duller than a cat's, and it cannot pull them into sheaths on its toes. Its feet are different because its ancestors hunted differently long, long ago. Wild dogs ran swiftly — much faster than cats. They chased their prey till it was tired out, then grabbed it with their big, curving teeth. A dog's claws are not used for catching food, so they don't need to be sharp.

WHAT IS SPACE?

SCIENTISTS have a special name for the moon and the stars and all the other objects in the sky — *celestial bodies*. There are billions of celestial bodies. All of them together make up the universe. And the part of the universe in between the celestial bodies is called space.

Does space go on beyond the farthest star? It is hard to imagine a celestial body that has nothing beyond it. Where does space end? It is hard to imagine a universe that has no limits. What shape could it have? Scientists don't yet know enough about space to answer such questions.

In the vast universe our earth is just a tiny speck in a bubble of air. And so when scientists talk about space they usually mean the part of the universe that is outside our atmosphere. That is why airplanes are not called spacecraft.

INDEX

Numerals in italics refer to pictures.
Entries printed in capital letters refer to question-titles.